If found, kindly return to:

Name: _____

Phone: _____

Greatly appreciated

THE STRESS-LESS LIFE GUIDE ADULTS

The simplest and most effective steps to a happier, healthier, and successful life!

CREATED BY
Dr. DIANNA M. and GABRIELLA K.
The Mother and Daughter Team

On top of our current monthly donations, a percentage of sales from ALL of our books will support children with mental and other health issues, some YouTube channels, and animal shelters which are helping abused and homeless animals.

Printed in the United States of America

First Printing, 2018

ISBN 978-1-7322971-0-4

Stress-Less Way Publishing

Connect with us:

Email: team@stresslessway.com
www.stresslessway.com

WELCOME!

The Mother and Daughter Team would like YOU to join us on the exciting journey to a Stress-Less Life!

Presented for your attention is a series of Guides with daily Journals for **ALL ages.** They will provide you with a practical step-by-step tool to facilitate inner peace, reduce your daily stress and lead to a more productive life.

Only together, with the help of **parents, close family members, teachers, and medical professionals,** can we build a safer environment for us, our children, and future generations.

OTHER GUIDES IN THIS SERIES:

- THE STRESS-LESS LIFE GUIDE - TEENS.
- THE STRESS-LESS LIFE GUIDE - SUMMERTIME OR ANYTIME - TEENS.
- THE STRESS-LESS LIFE GUIDE - KIDS AND PARENTS.
- THE STRESS-LESS LIFE GUIDE - SUMMERTIME OR ANYTIME - KIDS   AND PARENTS.

ENJOY OUR:

NEWEST AND ONGOING SERIES OF INCREDIBLY INSPIRING **STRESS-LESS COLORING BOOKS** FOR DIFFERENT AGES. These books include inspiring Quotes and Drawings from ACTUAL children and adults, some of whom have very challenging health issues.

Disclaimer

Presented below, The Stress-Less Life Guide was created for educational and learning purposes only. Our ultimate goal is to provide a useful aid for anyone, including parents, professionals, schoolteachers and doctors. It is never too late to be on the way to your own Stress-Less life. Integrating our practices and methods into your lives on a daily basis will allow you and your loved ones to cope with stress more intelligently. You will learn how to guide yourself to a more fulfilling and stressless life. You will be in charge of your health, happiness, and future success. By following these Guides, you will be inspired to share your newfound skills with many others along your path.

TABLE OF CONTENTS

FOREWORD

Hello fellow readers! It is a privilege to introduce you to the world of The Stress-Less Life Guides. My name is Dr. Anton Fisher, D.O. I am a licensed and Board Certified Psychiatrist. I was asked to review the contents of these books. Having done so, I wholeheartedly recommend them to readers of all ages.

Stress, which is Anxiety by another name, has always been difficult to treat. There are various known forms of psychotherapy recommended for stress, and they often involve journaling. This series of guides will help lead you on a path of self-discovery and understanding of the underlying factors of what is causing your stress. Completing the exercises in the journals will be an outlet for your negative emotions and help to deflate your stressors from your day. Some of these guides are meant for children or adolescents. Completing them together with a parent will help create or strengthen your family bond. The guides can also be completed on your own, with family, or in conjunction with a professional therapist.

I personally know the authors of these guides and the circumstances that led them to want to help our society at large. Their combined wisdom, experience, and unique perspectives helped create these journals.

This series of guides will introduce you to some of those rare books that can be a benefit to everyone. I am confident that following the exercises in these journals will lead to a reduction in anxiety/stress levels and improved functioning at work, school, home, and life in general.

Dr. Anton Fisher, D.O.

Dr. Anton Fisher, D.O. is a Board Certified Psychiatrist practicing in multiple states, including Nevada. He is the founder of **TeleMind™**, a novel telepsychiatry clinic located in the Las Vegas Valley and beyond. More information can be found at www.telemindclinic.com.

*Disclaimer: I do not have a financial interest in these guides. These guides are not a substitute for medical advice. If you believe you are experiencing symptoms of a mood, anxiety, attention or other disorder, please consult with a mental health professional. I waive any liability for the content or effects of these guides.

MY STORY...

Hi there!

My name is Dianna, and I am just an average human being with ordinary day-to-day problems. I am sure most of you can relate to that.

I am not a psychiatrist or a psychologist. I am not a writer. Actually, this is the first time in my life that I am publishing something - so, please have some mercy.

My ultimate goal is to try to create a peaceful, safe, and positive environment with less stress and cruelty in it for all of us and for future generations to come.

There are so many known ways to deal with stress: yoga, meditation, exercise, etc. I use them all on a regular basis and love them.

But **this Guide** will introduce you to an entirely new approach to stress management, with more stable and predictable results.

I am not claiming here that I will give you a magic pill and that **all** of your stress will vanish.
I do not promise anything to anyone!

But...
I can offer you my own amazing journey to a life with less stress and more happiness. I can share with you what helped me to take control of my own emotions. It worked for me - even though I am strongheaded - and hopefully it will work for you as well.

Yes, I am a Doctor (dentist). Also, I am a business owner, a mother, a wife, a sister, a grandma... The list is endless.

Nevertheless, I strongly believe it doesn't matter who you are or what you do; we are all going through the same stress, just with different silver linings.

Usually, the more responsibilities we all have, the more we stress.
The one thing I know for sure: I had a significant amount of stress during my whole life. Let me tell you - it was NOT fun. I am sure that most of us go through some stressful times daily and sometimes nightly as well.

I am not going to go in depth about the type of stress that I had to deal with every single day - not relevant here. Everyone has their own. What IS relevant - during one of those sleepless nights, a thought struck me.

I tried to recall the problems and concerns that I had to deal with a couple of weeks ago and even a couple of days ago. I just wanted to make sure they were resolved.

And guess what? **I was in shock!!!**

Most of them I couldn't even remember! **Some** of them were out of my control to begin with, so why bother?! **The rest** - were solved one way or another!

All the worrying, sleepless nights, and stress I had to go through were a waste of my precious time, and most importantly, **it took away from my health and happiness**!!!

Most of my problems were solved ANYWAY, **as always**, although mentally and physically, I was at a loss. I can never get that back...
I was so disappointed in myself that I had no control over my own mind and emotions.

Then I realized it doesn't matter if I am stressing out or not. Problems get resolved one way or another.

BINGO!!!
I had to stop the way I was **thinking about and reacting to** problems right then and there! I had to learn how to be in better control of my own mind, behavior, and life in general.
This is how and why The Stress-Less Life Guides were born!

P.S.

We need to learn how to separate REAL problems from imaginary ones. If you can't even recall what the fuss was about, the problem didn't even exist to begin with!

I firmly believe that stress is linked to poor health, anger, depression, and all the awful events happening in our world today. If I can only prevent something terrible or help someone enjoy their life to the fullest - my mission is accomplished.

I cannot tell you that I am 100% stress-free. I never will be. Life is very unpredictable.

But I can tell you one thing for sure. With the help of my journal, I am dealing with stress much better and handling my day-to-day life with more ease. And definitely sleeping better at night!

LOVE AND PEACE

"Clearly, stress is an inescapable part of life —
but it's important to understand it is *how you
deal with it* that will determine whether it will
translate into health problems later on. The
stress reaction should *dissipate* as quickly as
possible after the perceived danger has passed.
The scientific term for this is **resilience — the
ability of your body to rapidly return to normal,
both physically and emotionally, after a
stressful event**."

~Dr. Mercola

WHAT TO EXPECT

How this Journal will help manage/control your daily stress:

1. With daily practice, you will learn how to switch your thoughts from negative to positive in a matter of seconds. The saying "practice makes perfect" never gets old. It creates a simple habit that you will benefit from in your day-to-day life.

2. On worry-free days (fantastic!) you can write about positive events only. It would be nice to be able to go back in time and rehash those precious moments in the future.

3. Yes, YOU will have to be willing to step out of your comfort zone and still do all the work in the real world. No magic there. But remember, you always have those few precious seconds to switch to positive thoughts.

4. It is critical to make that switch fast. Our mind has a mind of its own and will try very hard to trick us into something less pleasant if we're too slow. I'm sharing this from my personal experience.

5. Daily practice in this Journal will help you to react and behave intelligently during difficult situations.

6. You will see that your "BIG" problem was not actually as big as time passes. You will understand how truly

insignificant the "problem" was. Your stress will be history, but **part of your health and happiness have been permanently stolen at that moment.**

7. "Time Heals"... The beauty of this journal is that you can always go back and see for yourself that all those worries were groundless, and most of your problems are probably resolved by now.
8. With time, you will gain better control over different situations and your mindful behavior.
9. You will handle your future problems with ease and reduced stress.

You will eventually understand that almost all these problems are temporary and will be resolved one way or another.

Remember - "Tomorrow is a better day".

The benefits that you will get from this Journal:

- You will be a happier and healthier person who will bring more positivity to the universe.
- You can share this knowledge with people you love and respect. You can teach them how to manage their stress. Consequently, you will be surrounded by positive people with similar values and become a part of a happy environment - "happy bubble" - a win-win situation.
- You will concentrate on who and what is actually important in your life.

- You will perform your daily tasks more efficiently with a full understanding that everything will be resolved sooner or later.
- You will be well conditioned to handle any future mishaps.

Life is too short to waste your time with stress and worries.

PRACTICE MAKES PERFECT

Steps to take daily or as needed:

The moment you feel stressed out or upset about something - **STOP: BECOME MINDFUL AND AWARE.** *Try to do the following:*

1. Limit your social media time to a minimum. Try to have a real face-to-face conversation with people you love and trust. Always remember YOU ARE NEVER ALONE with your problems and concerns! There is always someone around you who can help and guide you to proper solutions.

2. Tell yourself: "Tomorrow will be a better day, and my stress will be history. I am a healthy and happy individual." Even if you don't feel that way at that particular moment, make it your mantra/ affirmation. Tell yourself as many times as needed to clear your mind from any negativity. That alone is a great way to start thinking positive thoughts.

3. Go to that positive place in your mind when you're stressed. Put as many happy thoughts and pictures as you want in that space and use them as needed. You can create your own inspirational quotes/affirmations or use the

ones from my journal. You don't need many. **They have to be strong enough to serve as a switch from negative to positive.** That will be your way out from your "stress bubble."

4. Do what makes **YOU** happy.

Let me tell you about one of **MY** ways to deal with stress, which always puts me in a better mood.

I am addicted to a couple of YouTube channels. These are a few of them:

- Hope For Paws
- Vet Ranch
- Viktor Larkhill

It's unbelievable what people do to save animals! Also, it is so hard to believe how much cruelty there is in the world toward these helpless creatures. Every time I watch a new video, it melts my heart!

The end results are priceless. These abused animals find the place in their broken hearts to love and trust humans back again and again. I am always anxious to see the end. You finally get to see happy and healthy animals! That alone makes my day.

Check these channels out or find something to do for yourself that will make **YOU** happy.

P.S.
On top of our monthly donations, a percentage of sales from all my books will support some of those channels.

5. On a daily basis, at your convenience, write in this Journal the reason/reasons why you were stressed and what made your day better.

6. Give it some time (however much is needed- a day/two/a week) and revisit that page later.

You will be as shocked as I was. Most of those problems were probably solved by now. Stressing out was useless.

THAT IS IT!!!
A simple and effective way to control your emotions and stress levels. It works for me every time. I am sure it will work for you as well.

LOVE AND PEACE

"Our destiny changes with our thought; we shall become what we wish to become, do what we wish to do when our habitual thought corresponds with our desire."[4]

~Dr. Mercola

JOURNAL

"I cannot teach anybody anything. I can only make them think."

~Socrates

When you stay positive - you have the power over your circumstances; otherwise, the circumstances will have the power over you.

Date ___/___/20__

STRESSFUL MOMENTS:

_____

_____

_____

HAPPY MOMENTS:

_____

_____

_____

PLAN AHEAD TODAY TO MINIMIZE YOUR STRESS TOMORROW!
(OR YOU CAN JUST WRITE OR DRAW SOMETHING SILLY DOWN BELOW AND GO TO BED SMILING.)

PLANS FOR TOMORROW/TO DO LIST:

Each of us can allow or not allow daily events to cause stress. Without second guessing, we have to direct ourselves to something positive and stress-free mentally.

Date ___/___/20__

STRESSFUL MOMENTS:

_____

_____

_____

HAPPY MOMENTS:

_____

_____

_____

PLAN AHEAD TODAY TO MINIMIZE YOUR STRESS TOMORROW!

(OR YOU CAN JUST WRITE OR DRAW SOMETHING SILLY DOWN BELOW AND GO TO BED SMILING.)

PLANS FOR TOMORROW/TO DO LIST:

"Actively managing your stress levels with exercise, staying positive, connecting with others, engaging in hobbies, and spending time in nature is crucial for optimal health."(6) ~Dr. Mercola

Date ___/___/20__

STRESSFUL MOMENTS:

_____

_____

_____

HAPPY MOMENTS:

_____

_____

_____

PLAN AHEAD TODAY TO MINIMIZE YOUR STRESS TOMORROW!
(OR YOU CAN JUST WRITE OR DRAW SOMETHING SILLY DOWN BELOW AND GO TO BED SMILING.)
PLANS FOR TOMORROW/TO DO LIST:

"Learning to breathe mindfully can modify and accelerate your body's inherent self-regulating physiological and bioenergetic mechanisms. These changes are in large part due to the fact that you're oxygenating your body properly as well as correcting your internal and energetic balance, and it has a direct impact on your nervous system."(6)

~Dr. Mercola

Date ___/___/20__

STRESSFUL MOMENTS:

_____

_____

_____

HAPPY MOMENTS:

_____

_____

_____

PLAN AHEAD TODAY TO MINIMIZE YOUR STRESS TOMORROW!

(OR YOU CAN JUST WRITE OR DRAW SOMETHING SILLY DOWN BELOW AND GO TO BED SMILING.)

PLANS FOR TOMORROW/TO DO LIST:

"When you focus on problems, you will have more problems. When you focus on possibilities, you will have more opportunities."(10)

~unknown

Date ___/___/20__

STRESSFUL MOMENTS:

_____

_____

_____

HAPPY MOMENTS:

_____

_____

_____

PLAN AHEAD TODAY TO MINIMIZE YOUR STRESS TOMORROW!

(OR YOU CAN JUST WRITE OR DRAW SOMETHING SILLY DOWN BELOW AND GO TO BED SMILING.)

PLANS FOR TOMORROW/TO DO LIST:

"Engaging in a hobby gives you crucial time to play and simply enjoy yourself. A hobby can take your mind off of stress and adds more much-needed fun to your life."(6)

~Dr. Mercola

Date ___/___/20__

STRESSFUL MOMENTS:

_____

_____

_____

HAPPY MOMENTS:

_____

_____

_____

PLAN AHEAD TODAY TO MINIMIZE YOUR STRESS TOMORROW!
(OR YOU CAN JUST WRITE OR DRAW SOMETHING SILLY DOWN BELOW AND GO TO BED SMILING.)
PLANS FOR TOMORROW/TO DO LIST:

You have to exercise your mind like any other part of your body. You can't get strong or smart or flexible, etc. overnight. Training your mind into a positive direction takes time. The most important thing - IT IS UNDER YOUR CONTROL, AND YOU CAN START RIGHT HERE AND RIGHT NOW!

Date ___/___/20__

STRESSFUL MOMENTS:

_____

_____

_____

HAPPY MOMENTS:

_____

_____

_____

PLAN AHEAD TODAY TO MINIMIZE YOUR STRESS TOMORROW!

(OR YOU CAN JUST WRITE OR DRAW SOMETHING SILLY DOWN BELOW AND GO TO BED SMILING.)

PLANS FOR TOMORROW/TO DO LIST:

> **"A bad attitude is like a flat tire. You can't go anywhere till you change it."**(10)
>
> ~unknown

Date ___/___/20__

STRESSFUL MOMENTS:

_____

_____

_____

HAPPY MOMENTS:

_____

_____

_____

PLAN AHEAD TODAY TO MINIMIZE YOUR STRESS TOMORROW!

(OR YOU CAN JUST WRITE OR DRAW SOMETHING SILLY DOWN BELOW AND GO TO BED SMILING.)

PLANS FOR TOMORROW/TO DO LIST:

In every situation, always try to look on the bright side. The more you practice doing this, the faster you can direct your thoughts into a positive zone.

Date ___/___/20___

STRESSFUL MOMENTS:

_____

_____

_____

HAPPY MOMENTS:

_____

_____

_____

PLAN AHEAD TODAY TO MINIMIZE YOUR STRESS TOMORROW!
(OR YOU CAN JUST WRITE OR DRAW SOMETHING SILLY DOWN BELOW AND GO TO BED SMILING.)
PLANS FOR TOMORROW/TO DO LIST:

Get in touch with the cause of your stressful emotions. Think about what's upsetting you and why. Often, the situation, when inspected thoroughly, is actually somewhat different from what you've perceived. This alone can alleviate or even eliminate the stressor itself.

Date ___/___/20__

STRESSFUL MOMENTS:

_____

_____

_____

HAPPY MOMENTS:

_____

_____

_____

PLAN AHEAD TODAY TO MINIMIZE YOUR STRESS TOMORROW!

(OR YOU CAN JUST WRITE OR DRAW SOMETHING SILLY DOWN BELOW AND GO TO BED SMILING.)

PLANS FOR TOMORROW/TO DO LIST:

Try to deal with negativity by watching funny and cute YouTube videos. Never fails to put a smile on my face. The animals and babies videos are the best!

Date ___/___/20__

STRESSFUL MOMENTS:

_____

_____

_____

HAPPY MOMENTS:

_____

_____

_____

PLAN AHEAD TODAY TO MINIMIZE YOUR STRESS TOMORROW!
(OR YOU CAN JUST WRITE OR DRAW SOMETHING SILLY DOWN BELOW AND GO TO BED SMILING.)
PLANS FOR TOMORROW/TO DO LIST:

"Live in the very soul of expectation of better things, in the conviction that something large, grand, and beautiful will await you if your efforts are intelligent if your mind is kept in a creative condition and you struggle upward to your goal."(5)   ~O.S. Marden

Date ___/___/20__

STRESSFUL MOMENTS:

_____

_____

_____

HAPPY MOMENTS:

_____

_____

_____

PLAN AHEAD TODAY TO MINIMIZE YOUR STRESS TOMORROW!
(OR YOU CAN JUST WRITE OR DRAW SOMETHING SILLY DOWN BELOW AND GO TO BED SMILING.)

PLANS FOR TOMORROW/TO DO LIST:

When your body and mind are in balance, you will be ready for any challenge coming your way!

Date ___/___/20__

STRESSFUL MOMENTS:

_____

_____

_____

HAPPY MOMENTS:

_____

_____

_____

PLAN AHEAD TODAY TO MINIMIZE YOUR STRESS TOMORROW!
(OR YOU CAN JUST WRITE OR DRAW SOMETHING SILLY DOWN BELOW AND GO TO BED SMILING.)
PLANS FOR TOMORROW/TO DO LIST:

> **"The key to happiness is not to have what you want but to want what you have."**(9)
>
> ~Anonymous

Date ___/___/20___

STRESSFUL MOMENTS:

_____

_____

_____

HAPPY MOMENTS:

_____

_____

_____

PLAN AHEAD TODAY TO MINIMIZE YOUR STRESS TOMORROW!

(OR YOU CAN JUST WRITE OR DRAW SOMETHING SILLY DOWN BELOW AND GO TO BED SMILING.)

PLANS FOR TOMORROW/TO DO LIST:

"Be with those who bring out the best in you, not the stress in you."(10)

~unknown

Date ___/___/20__

STRESSFUL MOMENTS:

_____

_____

_____

HAPPY MOMENTS:

_____

_____

_____

PLAN AHEAD TODAY TO MINIMIZE YOUR STRESS TOMORROW!

(OR YOU CAN JUST WRITE OR DRAW SOMETHING SILLY DOWN BELOW AND GO TO BED SMILING.)

PLANS FOR TOMORROW/TO DO LIST:

"Laugh when you can, apologize when you should, and let go of what you can't change. Life's too short to be anything...but happy."(9)

~Anonymous

Date ___/___/20__

STRESSFUL MOMENTS:

_____

_____

_____

HAPPY MOMENTS:

_____

_____

_____

PLAN AHEAD TODAY TO MINIMIZE YOUR STRESS TOMORROW!
(OR YOU CAN JUST WRITE OR DRAW SOMETHING SILLY DOWN BELOW AND GO TO BED SMILING.)
PLANS FOR TOMORROW/TO DO LIST:

"The purpose of our lives is to be happy."(9)   ~Dalai Lama

Date ___/___/20__

STRESSFUL MOMENTS:

_____

_____

_____

HAPPY MOMENTS:

_____

_____

_____

PLAN AHEAD TODAY TO MINIMIZE YOUR STRESS TOMORROW!
(OR YOU CAN JUST WRITE OR DRAW SOMETHING SILLY DOWN BELOW AND GO TO BED SMILING.)
PLANS FOR TOMORROW/TO DO LIST:

As soon as you wake up, announce out loud what kind of day you want to have today. And then don't forget to follow through.

Date ___/___/20__

STRESSFUL MOMENTS:

_____

_____

_____

HAPPY MOMENTS:

_____

_____

_____

PLAN AHEAD TODAY TO MINIMIZE YOUR STRESS TOMORROW!
(OR YOU CAN JUST WRITE OR DRAW SOMETHING SILLY DOWN BELOW AND GO TO BED SMILING.)
PLANS FOR TOMORROW/TO DO LIST:

"The most difficult phase of life is not when no one understands you; it is when you don't understand yourself."(9)   ~Anonymous

Date ___/___/20__

STRESSFUL MOMENTS:

_____

_____

_____

HAPPY MOMENTS:

_____

_____

_____

PLAN AHEAD TODAY TO MINIMIZE YOUR STRESS TOMORROW!

(OR YOU CAN JUST WRITE OR DRAW SOMETHING SILLY DOWN BELOW AND GO TO BED SMILING.)

PLANS FOR TOMORROW/TO DO LIST:

Negative people attract negativity. Positive people attract positivity. Surround yourself with positive ones, and lose the others.

Date ___ / ___ /20___

STRESSFUL MOMENTS:

_____

_____

_____

HAPPY MOMENTS:

_____

_____

_____

PLAN AHEAD TODAY TO MINIMIZE YOUR STRESS TOMORROW!

(OR YOU CAN JUST WRITE OR DRAW SOMETHING SILLY DOWN BELOW AND GO TO BED SMILING.)

PLANS FOR TOMORROW/TO DO LIST:

Waking up in the morning and thinking about what you are grateful for is so important. Start listing in your head what you are thankful for TODAY. This is a great habit that will fill you with positive energy for the rest of the day.

Date ___/___/20__

STRESSFUL MOMENTS:

_____

_____

_____

HAPPY MOMENTS:

_____

_____

_____

PLAN AHEAD TODAY TO MINIMIZE YOUR STRESS TOMORROW!
(OR YOU CAN JUST WRITE OR DRAW SOMETHING SILLY DOWN BELOW AND GO TO BED SMILING.)
PLANS FOR TOMORROW/TO DO LIST:

"Every day may not be good, but there is something good in every day."(2)

~unknown

Date ___/___/20__

STRESSFUL MOMENTS:

_____

_____

_____

HAPPY MOMENTS:

_____

_____

_____

PLAN AHEAD TODAY TO MINIMIZE YOUR STRESS TOMORROW!
(OR YOU CAN JUST WRITE OR DRAW SOMETHING SILLY DOWN BELOW AND GO TO BED SMILING.)

PLANS FOR TOMORROW/TO DO LIST:

"Only put off until tomorrow what you are willing to die having left undone."(9)

~Pablo Picasso

Date ___/___/20__

STRESSFUL MOMENTS:

_____

_____

_____

HAPPY MOMENTS:

_____

_____

_____

PLAN AHEAD TODAY TO MINIMIZE YOUR STRESS TOMORROW!

(OR YOU CAN JUST WRITE OR DRAW SOMETHING SILLY DOWN BELOW AND GO TO BED SMILING.)

PLANS FOR TOMORROW/TO DO LIST:

Having contagious positive energy and a "can do attitude" is a vital ingredient for your success.

Date ___ / ___ /20 ___

STRESSFUL MOMENTS:

_____

_____

_____

HAPPY MOMENTS:

_____

_____

_____

PLAN AHEAD TODAY TO MINIMIZE YOUR STRESS TOMORROW!

(OR YOU CAN JUST WRITE OR DRAW SOMETHING SILLY DOWN BELOW AND GO TO BED SMILING.)

PLANS FOR TOMORROW/TO DO LIST:

Try to perform random acts of kindness. They give you a lasting feel-good factor.

Date ___/___/20__

STRESSFUL MOMENTS:

_____

_____

_____

HAPPY MOMENTS:

_____

_____

_____

PLAN AHEAD TODAY TO MINIMIZE YOUR STRESS TOMORROW!

(OR YOU CAN JUST WRITE OR DRAW SOMETHING SILLY DOWN BELOW AND GO TO BED SMILING.)

PLANS FOR TOMORROW/TO DO LIST:

"I cannot teach anybody anything. I can only make them think."(5)

~Socrates

Date ___/___/20___

STRESSFUL MOMENTS:

_____

_____

_____

HAPPY MOMENTS:

_____

_____

_____

PLAN AHEAD TODAY TO MINIMIZE YOUR STRESS TOMORROW!

(OR YOU CAN JUST WRITE OR DRAW SOMETHING SILLY DOWN BELOW AND GO TO BED SMILING.)

PLANS FOR TOMORROW/TO DO LIST:

"I've had a lot of worries in my life, most of which never happened."(10)

~Mark Twain

Date ___/___/20__

STRESSFUL MOMENTS:

_____

_____

_____

HAPPY MOMENTS:

_____

_____

_____

PLAN AHEAD TODAY TO MINIMIZE YOUR STRESS TOMORROW!

(OR YOU CAN JUST WRITE OR DRAW SOMETHING SILLY DOWN BELOW AND GO TO BED SMILING.)

PLANS FOR TOMORROW/TO DO LIST:

"We can complain because rose bushes have thorns or rejoice because thorn bushes have roses."(5)   ~Abraham Lincoln

Date ___/___/20__

STRESSFUL MOMENTS:

_____

_____

_____

HAPPY MOMENTS:

_____

_____

_____

PLAN AHEAD TODAY TO MINIMIZE YOUR STRESS TOMORROW!

(OR YOU CAN JUST WRITE OR DRAW SOMETHING SILLY DOWN BELOW AND GO TO BED SMILING.)

PLANS FOR TOMORROW/TO DO LIST:

"To handle yourself, use your head; to handle others, use your heart."(5)

~Eleanor Roosevelt

Date ___/___/20__

STRESSFUL MOMENTS:

_____

_____

_____

HAPPY MOMENTS:

_____

_____

_____

PLAN AHEAD TODAY TO MINIMIZE YOUR STRESS TOMORROW!

(OR YOU CAN JUST WRITE OR DRAW SOMETHING SILLY DOWN BELOW AND GO TO BED SMILING.)

PLANS FOR TOMORROW/TO DO LIST:

"You may delay, but time will not."(5) ~Benjamin Franklin

Date ___/___/20__

STRESSFUL MOMENTS:

_____

_____

_____

HAPPY MOMENTS:

_____

_____

_____

PLAN AHEAD TODAY TO MINIMIZE YOUR STRESS TOMORROW!

(OR YOU CAN JUST WRITE OR DRAW SOMETHING SILLY DOWN BELOW AND GO TO BED SMILING.)

PLANS FOR TOMORROW/TO DO LIST:

"Tell me, and I forget. Teach me, and I may remember. Involve me, and I learn."(5)

~Benjamin Franklin

Date ___/___/20__

STRESSFUL MOMENTS:

_____

_____

_____

HAPPY MOMENTS:

_____

_____

_____

PLAN AHEAD TODAY TO MINIMIZE YOUR STRESS TOMORROW!
(OR YOU CAN JUST WRITE OR DRAW SOMETHING SILLY DOWN BELOW AND GO TO BED SMILING.)
PLANS FOR TOMORROW/TO DO LIST:

Beware - some so-called friends can drain you of your energy. Distance yourself from those types of people. You don't have to answer the phone or the door every time they call. Create your own "positive bubble".

Date ___/___/20___

STRESSFUL MOMENTS:

_____

_____

_____

HAPPY MOMENTS:

_____

_____

_____

PLAN AHEAD TODAY TO MINIMIZE YOUR STRESS TOMORROW!

(OR YOU CAN JUST WRITE OR DRAW SOMETHING SILLY DOWN BELOW AND GO TO BED SMILING.)

PLANS FOR TOMORROW/TO DO LIST:

"Those who are optimistic have an easier time dealing with stress and are more inclined to open themselves up to opportunities to have positive regenerative experiences."(6)   ~Dr. Mercola

Date ___/___/20__

STRESSFUL MOMENTS:

_____

_____

_____

HAPPY MOMENTS:

_____

_____

_____

PLAN AHEAD TODAY TO MINIMIZE YOUR STRESS TOMORROW!
(OR YOU CAN JUST WRITE OR DRAW SOMETHING SILLY DOWN BELOW AND GO TO BED SMILING.)
PLANS FOR TOMORROW/TO DO LIST:

"Loneliness can be a major source of stress, so make a point to connect with those around you – even a quick chat while in line at the grocery store. Work your way up to volunteering, attending community events, meeting acquaintances for coffee, or taking a class to meet others with like interests."(6)   ~Dr. Mercola

Date ___ / ___ /20 __

STRESSFUL MOMENTS:

_____

_____

_____

HAPPY MOMENTS:

_____

_____

_____

PLAN AHEAD TODAY TO MINIMIZE YOUR STRESS TOMORROW!
(OR YOU CAN JUST WRITE OR DRAW SOMETHING SILLY DOWN BELOW AND GO TO BED SMILING.)
PLANS FOR TOMORROW/TO DO LIST:

> "Taking even 10 minutes to sit quietly and shut out the chaos around you can trigger your relaxation response. Meditating during your breaks can help you to decrease feelings of stress and anxiety even more."(6)
> ~Dr. Mercola

Date ___/___/20__

STRESSFUL MOMENTS:

_____

_____

_____

HAPPY MOMENTS:

_____

_____

_____

PLAN AHEAD TODAY TO MINIMIZE YOUR STRESS TOMORROW!
(OR YOU CAN JUST WRITE OR DRAW SOMETHING SILLY DOWN BELOW AND GO TO BED SMILING.)
PLANS FOR TOMORROW/TO DO LIST:

"Nothing gives one person so much advantage over another as to remain always cool and unruffled under all circumstances."(5)

~Thomas Jefferson

Date ___/___/20__

STRESSFUL MOMENTS:

_____

_____

_____

HAPPY MOMENTS:

_____

_____

_____

PLAN AHEAD TODAY TO MINIMIZE YOUR STRESS TOMORROW!
(OR YOU CAN JUST WRITE OR DRAW SOMETHING SILLY DOWN BELOW AND GO TO BED SMILING.)
PLANS FOR TOMORROW/TO DO LIST:

"Years of love have been forgotten in the hatred of a minute."(5)

~Edgar Allan Poe

Date ___/___/20__

STRESSFUL MOMENTS:

_____

_____

_____

HAPPY MOMENTS:

_____

_____

_____

PLAN AHEAD TODAY TO MINIMIZE YOUR STRESS TOMORROW!
(OR YOU CAN JUST WRITE OR DRAW SOMETHING SILLY DOWN BELOW AND GO TO BED SMILING.)
PLANS FOR TOMORROW/TO DO LIST:

"The way to change others' minds is with affection and not anger."(5)

Date ___/___/20__

STRESSFUL MOMENTS:

_____

_____

_____

HAPPY MOMENTS:

_____

_____

_____

PLAN AHEAD TODAY TO MINIMIZE YOUR STRESS TOMORROW!

(OR YOU CAN JUST WRITE OR DRAW SOMETHING SILLY DOWN BELOW AND GO TO BED SMILING.)

PLANS FOR TOMORROW/TO DO LIST:

"We can never obtain peace in the outer world until we make peace with ourselves."(5)

~Dalai Lama

Date ___/___/20__

STRESSFUL MOMENTS:

_____

_____

_____

HAPPY MOMENTS:

_____

_____

_____

PLAN AHEAD TODAY TO MINIMIZE YOUR STRESS TOMORROW!
(OR YOU CAN JUST WRITE OR DRAW SOMETHING SILLY DOWN BELOW AND GO TO BED SMILING.)
PLANS FOR TOMORROW/TO DO LIST:

"Remember that sometimes not getting what you want is a wonderful stroke of luck."(5)

~ Dalai Lama

Date ___/___/20___

STRESSFUL MOMENTS:

_____

_____

_____

HAPPY MOMENTS:

_____

_____

_____

PLAN AHEAD TODAY TO MINIMIZE YOUR STRESS TOMORROW!

(OR YOU CAN JUST WRITE OR DRAW SOMETHING SILLY DOWN BELOW AND GO TO BED SMILING.)

PLANS FOR TOMORROW/TO DO LIST:

"It's a new day, fresh start, fresh energy, new opportunities. Get your mind right, be thankful, be positive and start your day right."(10)

~unknown

Date ___/___/20__

STRESSFUL MOMENTS:

_____

_____

_____

HAPPY MOMENTS:

_____

_____

_____

PLAN AHEAD TODAY TO MINIMIZE YOUR STRESS TOMORROW!

(OR YOU CAN JUST WRITE OR DRAW SOMETHING SILLY DOWN BELOW AND GO TO BED SMILING.)

PLANS FOR TOMORROW/TO DO LIST:

Self-belief, self-love, persistence, hard work, positive thinking - it's all attitude. The right attitude has the power to shape the course of your life and the quality of your experiences.

Date ___/___/20__

STRESSFUL MOMENTS:

_____

_____

_____

HAPPY MOMENTS:

_____

_____

_____

PLAN AHEAD TODAY TO MINIMIZE YOUR STRESS TOMORROW!

(OR YOU CAN JUST WRITE OR DRAW SOMETHING SILLY DOWN BELOW AND GO TO BED SMILING.)

PLANS FOR TOMORROW/TO DO LIST:

"Silence is sometimes the best answer."(5) ~Dalai Lama

Date ___/___/20__

STRESSFUL MOMENTS:

_____

_____

_____

HAPPY MOMENTS:

_____

_____

_____

PLAN AHEAD TODAY TO MINIMIZE YOUR STRESS TOMORROW!
(OR YOU CAN JUST WRITE OR DRAW SOMETHING SILLY DOWN BELOW AND GO TO BED SMILING.)
PLANS FOR TOMORROW/TO DO LIST:

"**Happiness is not something ready-made. It comes from your own actions.**"(5)

~Dalai Lama

Date ___/___/20__

STRESSFUL MOMENTS:

_____

_____

_____

HAPPY MOMENTS:

_____

_____

_____

PLAN AHEAD TODAY TO MINIMIZE YOUR STRESS TOMORROW!
(OR YOU CAN JUST WRITE OR DRAW SOMETHING SILLY DOWN BELOW AND GO TO BED SMILING.)
PLANS FOR TOMORROW/TO DO LIST:

"Writing down how you're feeling - that helps tremendously! You can expel all your thoughts and feelings (positive and negative) so they're out in the open and not bottled up inside. Definitely a stress reliever."(10)

Date ___/___/20__

STRESSFUL MOMENTS:

_____

_____

_____

HAPPY MOMENTS:

_____

_____

_____

PLAN AHEAD TODAY TO MINIMIZE YOUR STRESS TOMORROW!

(OR YOU CAN JUST WRITE OR DRAW SOMETHING SILLY DOWN BELOW AND GO TO BED SMILING.)

PLANS FOR TOMORROW/TO DO LIST:

"Let no one ever come to you without leaving better and happier."(5)

~Mother Teresa

Date ___/___/20__

STRESSFUL MOMENTS:

_____

_____

_____

HAPPY MOMENTS:

_____

_____

_____

PLAN AHEAD TODAY TO MINIMIZE YOUR STRESS TOMORROW!

(OR YOU CAN JUST WRITE OR DRAW SOMETHING SILLY DOWN BELOW AND GO TO BED SMILING.)

PLANS FOR TOMORROW/TO DO LIST:

"Yesterday is gone. Tomorrow has not yet come. We have only today. Let us begin."(5)

~Mother Teresa

Date ___/___/20__

STRESSFUL MOMENTS:

_____

_____

_____

HAPPY MOMENTS:

_____

_____

_____

PLAN AHEAD TODAY TO MINIMIZE YOUR STRESS TOMORROW!

(OR YOU CAN JUST WRITE OR DRAW SOMETHING SILLY DOWN BELOW AND GO TO BED SMILING.)

PLANS FOR TOMORROW/TO DO LIST:

"Stress is very much like a snowball rolling down a mountain, gaining momentum, gaining speed and growing until suddenly it crashes. That crash, unfortunately, is often at the expense of your health."(7)

~Dr. Mercola

Date ___/___/20__

STRESSFUL MOMENTS:

_____

_____

_____

HAPPY MOMENTS:

_____

_____

_____

PLAN AHEAD TODAY TO MINIMIZE YOUR STRESS TOMORROW!

(OR YOU CAN JUST WRITE OR DRAW SOMETHING SILLY DOWN BELOW AND GO TO BED SMILING.)

PLANS FOR TOMORROW/TO DO LIST:

"Happiness depends upon ourselves."(5)   ~Aristotle

Date ___/___/20__

STRESSFUL MOMENTS:

_____

_____

_____

HAPPY MOMENTS:

_____

_____

_____

PLAN AHEAD TODAY TO MINIMIZE YOUR STRESS TOMORROW!
(OR YOU CAN JUST WRITE OR DRAW SOMETHING SILLY DOWN BELOW AND GO TO BED SMILING.)
PLANS FOR TOMORROW/TO DO LIST:

"Happiness is the meaning and the purpose of life, the whole aim, and end of human existence."(5)

~Aristotle

Date ___/___/20__

STRESSFUL MOMENTS:

_____

_____

_____

HAPPY MOMENTS:

_____

_____

_____

PLAN AHEAD TODAY TO MINIMIZE YOUR STRESS TOMORROW!
(OR YOU CAN JUST WRITE OR DRAW SOMETHING SILLY DOWN BELOW AND GO TO BED SMILING.)

PLANS FOR TOMORROW/TO DO LIST:

"Love all, trust a few, do wrong to none."(5)   ~William Shakespeare

Date ___/___/20__

STRESSFUL MOMENTS:

_____

_____

_____

HAPPY MOMENTS:

_____

_____

_____

PLAN AHEAD TODAY TO MINIMIZE YOUR STRESS TOMORROW!
(OR YOU CAN JUST WRITE OR DRAW SOMETHING SILLY DOWN BELOW AND GO TO BED SMILING.)
PLANS FOR TOMORROW/TO DO LIST:

"A friend to all is a friend to none."(5) ~Aristotle

Date ___/___/20__

STRESSFUL MOMENTS:

_____

_____

_____

HAPPY MOMENTS:

_____

_____

_____

PLAN AHEAD TODAY TO MINIMIZE YOUR STRESS TOMORROW!

(OR YOU CAN JUST WRITE OR DRAW SOMETHING SILLY DOWN BELOW AND GO TO BED SMILING.)

PLANS FOR TOMORROW/TO DO LIST:

"Never allow someone to be your priority while allowing yourself to be their option."(5)

~Mark Twain

Date ___/___/20__

STRESSFUL MOMENTS:

_____

_____

_____

HAPPY MOMENTS:

_____

_____

_____

PLAN AHEAD TODAY TO MINIMIZE YOUR STRESS TOMORROW!

(OR YOU CAN JUST WRITE OR DRAW SOMETHING SILLY DOWN BELOW AND GO TO BED SMILING.)

PLANS FOR TOMORROW/TO DO LIST:

> "Keep away from people who try to belittle your ambitions. Small people always do that, but the really great make you feel that you, too, can become great."(5)
>
> ~Mark Twain

Date ___/___/20__

STRESSFUL MOMENTS:

_____

_____

_____

HAPPY MOMENTS:

_____

_____

_____

PLAN AHEAD TODAY TO MINIMIZE YOUR STRESS TOMORROW!

(OR YOU CAN JUST WRITE OR DRAW SOMETHING SILLY DOWN BELOW AND GO TO BED SMILING.)

PLANS FOR TOMORROW/TO DO LIST:

A positive attitude is the only way to happiness.

Date ___/___/20__

STRESSFUL MOMENTS:

_____

_____

_____

HAPPY MOMENTS:

_____

_____

_____

PLAN AHEAD TODAY TO MINIMIZE YOUR STRESS TOMORROW!
(OR YOU CAN JUST WRITE OR DRAW SOMETHING SILLY DOWN BELOW AND GO TO BED SMILING.)
PLANS FOR TOMORROW/TO DO LIST:

"If you tell the truth, you don't have to remember anything."(5)

. ~Mark Twain

Date ___/___/20__

STRESSFUL MOMENTS:

_____

_____

_____

HAPPY MOMENTS:

_____

_____

_____

PLAN AHEAD TODAY TO MINIMIZE YOUR STRESS TOMORROW!

(OR YOU CAN JUST WRITE OR DRAW SOMETHING SILLY DOWN BELOW AND GO TO BED SMILING.)

PLANS FOR TOMORROW/TO DO LIST:

"There is nothing either good or bad, but thinking makes it so."(5)

~William Shakespeare

Date ___/___/20__

STRESSFUL MOMENTS:

_____

_____

_____

HAPPY MOMENTS:

_____

_____

_____

PLAN AHEAD TODAY TO MINIMIZE YOUR STRESS TOMORROW!

(OR YOU CAN JUST WRITE OR DRAW SOMETHING SILLY DOWN BELOW AND GO TO BED SMILING.)

PLANS FOR TOMORROW/TO DO LIST:

"It is not in the stars to hold our destiny but in ourselves."(5)

~William Shakespeare

Date ___/___/20__

STRESSFUL MOMENTS:

_____

_____

_____

HAPPY MOMENTS:

_____

_____

_____

PLAN AHEAD TODAY TO MINIMIZE YOUR STRESS TOMORROW!
(OR YOU CAN JUST WRITE OR DRAW SOMETHING SILLY DOWN BELOW AND GO TO BED SMILING.)
PLANS FOR TOMORROW/TO DO LIST:

Try to focus on *just today*. Do not worry about what tomorrow will be like. Concentrating on just today seems to limit potential stress and anxiety.

Date ___ / ___ /20__

STRESSFUL MOMENTS:

_____

_____

_____

HAPPY MOMENTS:

_____

_____

_____

PLAN AHEAD TODAY TO MINIMIZE YOUR STRESS TOMORROW!
(OR YOU CAN JUST WRITE OR DRAW SOMETHING SILLY DOWN BELOW AND GO TO BED SMILING.)
PLANS FOR TOMORROW/TO DO LIST:

Spend some time playing with your pets or go to a pet store. Their unconditional love can be such a great comfort.

Date ___/___/20___

STRESSFUL MOMENTS:

_____

_____

_____

HAPPY MOMENTS:

_____

_____

_____

PLAN AHEAD TODAY TO MINIMIZE YOUR STRESS TOMORROW!
(OR YOU CAN JUST WRITE OR DRAW SOMETHING SILLY DOWN BELOW AND GO TO BED SMILING.)
PLANS FOR TOMORROW/TO DO LIST:

"Be not afraid of greatness. Some are born great, some achieve greatness, and others have greatness thrust upon them."(5)

~William Shakespeare

Date ___/___/20__

STRESSFUL MOMENTS:

_____

_____

_____

HAPPY MOMENTS:

_____

_____

_____

PLAN AHEAD TODAY TO MINIMIZE YOUR STRESS TOMORROW!

(OR YOU CAN JUST WRITE OR DRAW SOMETHING SILLY DOWN BELOW AND GO TO BED SMILING.)

PLANS FOR TOMORROW/TO DO LIST:

When you feel a negative emotion, accept it, and then remind yourself that as time passes, so will that negative feeling.

Date ___/___/20__

STRESSFUL MOMENTS:

_____

_____

_____

HAPPY MOMENTS:

_____

_____

_____

PLAN AHEAD TODAY TO MINIMIZE YOUR STRESS TOMORROW!
(OR YOU CAN JUST WRITE OR DRAW SOMETHING SILLY DOWN BELOW AND GO TO BED SMILING.)
PLANS FOR TOMORROW/TO DO LIST:

"Practice forgiveness. It will improve quality of your life and it is essential to your happiness, health, mind, and inner peace."(10)

~unknown

Date ___/___/20__

STRESSFUL MOMENTS:

_____

_____

_____

HAPPY MOMENTS:

_____

_____

_____

PLAN AHEAD TODAY TO MINIMIZE YOUR STRESS TOMORROW!
(OR YOU CAN JUST WRITE OR DRAW SOMETHING SILLY DOWN BELOW AND GO TO BED SMILING.)

PLANS FOR TOMORROW/TO DO LIST:

"Progress is impossible without change, and those who cannot change their minds cannot change anything."(1)   ~Bernard Shaw

Date ___/___/20___

STRESSFUL MOMENTS:

_____

_____

_____

HAPPY MOMENTS:

_____

_____

_____

PLAN AHEAD TODAY TO MINIMIZE YOUR STRESS TOMORROW!

(OR YOU CAN JUST WRITE OR DRAW SOMETHING SILLY DOWN BELOW AND GO TO BED SMILING.)

PLANS FOR TOMORROW/TO DO LIST:

Practice self-love daily. Believe in yourself. Negative thoughts are like passing clouds. Exercise your mind to concentrate on the positive in your life.

Date ___/___/20__

STRESSFUL MOMENTS:

_____

_____

_____

HAPPY MOMENTS:

_____

_____

_____

PLAN AHEAD TODAY TO MINIMIZE YOUR STRESS TOMORROW!
(OR YOU CAN JUST WRITE OR DRAW SOMETHING SILLY DOWN BELOW AND GO TO BED SMILING.)
PLANS FOR TOMORROW/TO DO LIST:

Believe in yourself. Do not give up on your dreams or goals. The journey is going to be hard and unpredictable, but never give up.

Date ___ / ___ /20__

STRESSFUL MOMENTS:

_____

_____

_____

HAPPY MOMENTS:

_____

_____

_____

PLAN AHEAD TODAY TO MINIMIZE YOUR STRESS TOMORROW!
(OR YOU CAN JUST WRITE OR DRAW SOMETHING SILLY DOWN BELOW AND GO TO BED SMILING.)
PLANS FOR TOMORROW/TO DO LIST:

The only way you will be able to change your world is by changing your thoughts and attitude.

Date ___/___/20__

STRESSFUL MOMENTS:

_____

_____

_____

HAPPY MOMENTS:

_____

_____

_____

PLAN AHEAD TODAY TO MINIMIZE YOUR STRESS TOMORROW!
(OR YOU CAN JUST WRITE OR DRAW SOMETHING SILLY DOWN BELOW AND GO TO BED SMILING.)
PLANS FOR TOMORROW/TO DO LIST:

"Try to do one thing every single day to make your life more enjoyable. Whether it be to clean your car or to invite your loved ones for dinner, just do one thing. Three hundred and sixty-five days in a year!! You do the math. This really works, and it WILL shift your life into a positive mode."(10)

~unknown

Date ___/___/20__

STRESSFUL MOMENTS:

_____

_____

_____

HAPPY MOMENTS:

_____

_____

_____

PLAN AHEAD TODAY TO MINIMIZE YOUR STRESS TOMORROW!
(OR YOU CAN JUST WRITE OR DRAW SOMETHING SILLY DOWN BELOW AND GO TO BED SMILING.)
PLANS FOR TOMORROW/TO DO LIST:

Remember, just because you think a thought, doesn't necessarily mean it is true. So, stop stressing out about possibly nothing.

Date ___/___/20__

STRESSFUL MOMENTS:

_____

_____

_____

HAPPY MOMENTS:

_____

_____

_____

PLAN AHEAD TODAY TO MINIMIZE YOUR STRESS TOMORROW!
(OR YOU CAN JUST WRITE OR DRAW SOMETHING SILLY DOWN BELOW AND GO TO BED SMILING.)
PLANS FOR TOMORROW/TO DO LIST:

Positive thinking is very contagious and addictive. You will become a human magnet for positive people. You will create your own "happy bubble".

Date ___/___/20__

STRESSFUL MOMENTS:

_____

_____

_____

HAPPY MOMENTS:

_____

_____

_____

PLAN AHEAD TODAY TO MINIMIZE YOUR STRESS TOMORROW!

(OR YOU CAN JUST WRITE OR DRAW SOMETHING SILLY DOWN BELOW AND GO TO BED SMILING.)

PLANS FOR TOMORROW/TO DO LIST:

"No one saves us but ourselves. No one can and no one may. We ourselves must walk the path."(9)   ~The Buddha

Date ___/___/20__

STRESSFUL MOMENTS:

_____

_____

_____

HAPPY MOMENTS:

_____

_____

_____

PLAN AHEAD TODAY TO MINIMIZE YOUR STRESS TOMORROW!
(OR YOU CAN JUST WRITE OR DRAW SOMETHING SILLY DOWN BELOW AND GO TO BED SMILING.)
PLANS FOR TOMORROW/TO DO LIST:

"Our problems are man-made. Therefore, they may be solved by man. And man can be as big as he wants. No problem of human destiny is beyond human beings."(5)   ~John F. Kennedy

Date ___ / ___ /20__

STRESSFUL MOMENTS:

_____

_____

_____

HAPPY MOMENTS:

_____

_____

_____

PLAN AHEAD TODAY TO MINIMIZE YOUR STRESS TOMORROW!

(OR YOU CAN JUST WRITE OR DRAW SOMETHING SILLY DOWN BELOW AND GO TO BED SMILING.)

PLANS FOR TOMORROW/TO DO LIST:

> "Peace is a daily, a weekly, a monthly process, gradually changing opinions, slowly eroding old barriers, quietly building new structures."(5)
>
> ~J. F. Kennedy

Date ___/___/20__

STRESSFUL MOMENTS:

_____

_____

_____

HAPPY MOMENTS:

_____

_____

_____

PLAN AHEAD TODAY TO MINIMIZE YOUR STRESS TOMORROW!
(OR YOU CAN JUST WRITE OR DRAW SOMETHING SILLY DOWN BELOW AND GO TO BED SMILING.)

PLANS FOR TOMORROW/TO DO LIST:

"Nothing gives one person so much advantage over another
as to remain always cool and unruffled under all circumstances."(9)

~Thomas Jefferson

Date ___/___/20___

STRESSFUL MOMENTS:

_____

_____

_____

HAPPY MOMENTS:

_____

_____

_____

**PLAN AHEAD TODAY TO MINIMIZE YOUR STRESS
TOMORROW!**
(OR YOU CAN JUST WRITE OR DRAW SOMETHING SILLY DOWN BELOW AND
GO TO BED SMILING.)
PLANS FOR TOMORROW/TO DO LIST:

You should never let your mind wander into the negative-thoughts zone. Commit to stay focused on happiness and live in the present moment. Yesterday is gone. Tomorrow is not guaranteed. Enjoy your life today!

Date ___/___/20__

STRESSFUL MOMENTS:

_____

_____

_____

HAPPY MOMENTS:

_____

_____

_____

PLAN AHEAD TODAY TO MINIMIZE YOUR STRESS TOMORROW!
(OR YOU CAN JUST WRITE OR DRAW SOMETHING SILLY DOWN BELOW AND GO TO BED SMILING.)
PLANS FOR TOMORROW/TO DO LIST:

"The greatest weapon against stress is your ability to choose one thought over another."(10)

~William James

Date ___/___/20__

STRESSFUL MOMENTS:

_____

_____

_____

HAPPY MOMENTS:

_____

_____

_____

PLAN AHEAD TODAY TO MINIMIZE YOUR STRESS TOMORROW!

(OR YOU CAN JUST WRITE OR DRAW SOMETHING SILLY DOWN BELOW AND GO TO BED SMILING.)

PLANS FOR TOMORROW/TO DO LIST:

Don't let your mind be your limitation. Learn about the power of your mind and stay in control. Limit negativity around you. Focus on your happiness and positive attitude.

Date ___/___/20__

STRESSFUL MOMENTS:

_____

_____

_____

HAPPY MOMENTS:

_____

_____

_____

PLAN AHEAD TODAY TO MINIMIZE YOUR STRESS TOMORROW!

(OR YOU CAN JUST WRITE OR DRAW SOMETHING SILLY DOWN BELOW AND GO TO BED SMILING.)

PLANS FOR TOMORROW/TO DO LIST:

"People are just as happy as they make up their minds to be."(10)

~Abraham Lincoln

Date ___/___/20__

STRESSFUL MOMENTS:

_____

_____

_____

HAPPY MOMENTS:

_____

_____

_____

PLAN AHEAD TODAY TO MINIMIZE YOUR STRESS TOMORROW!

(OR YOU CAN JUST WRITE OR DRAW SOMETHING SILLY DOWN BELOW AND GO TO BED SMILING.)

PLANS FOR TOMORROW/TO DO LIST:

"Happiness doesn't depend on any external conditions. It is governed by our mental attitude."(5)

~Dale Carnegie

Date ___/___/20__

STRESSFUL MOMENTS:

_____

_____

_____

HAPPY MOMENTS:

_____

_____

_____

PLAN AHEAD TODAY TO MINIMIZE YOUR STRESS TOMORROW!

(OR YOU CAN JUST WRITE OR DRAW SOMETHING SILLY DOWN BELOW AND GO TO BED SMILING.)

PLANS FOR TOMORROW/TO DO LIST:

> **"Happiness depends more on the inward disposition of mind than on outward circumstances."**(9)
> ~Benjamin Franklin

Date ___/___/20___

STRESSFUL MOMENTS:

_____

_____

_____

HAPPY MOMENTS:

_____

_____

_____

PLAN AHEAD TODAY TO MINIMIZE YOUR STRESS TOMORROW!

(OR YOU CAN JUST WRITE OR DRAW SOMETHING SILLY DOWN BELOW AND GO TO BED SMILING.)

PLANS FOR TOMORROW/TO DO LIST:

> "Whenever you're in conflict with someone, there is one factor that can make the difference between damaging your relationship and deepening it. That factor is an attitude."(5)   ~William James

Date ___/___/20___

STRESSFUL MOMENTS:

_____

_____

_____

HAPPY MOMENTS:

_____

_____

_____

PLAN AHEAD TODAY TO MINIMIZE YOUR STRESS TOMORROW!

(OR YOU CAN JUST WRITE OR DRAW SOMETHING SILLY DOWN BELOW AND GO TO BED SMILING.)

PLANS FOR TOMORROW/TO DO LIST:

"Attitude is a little thing that makes a big difference."(9)

~Winston Churchill

Date ___/___/20__

STRESSFUL MOMENTS:

_____

_____

_____

HAPPY MOMENTS:

_____

_____

_____

PLAN AHEAD TODAY TO MINIMIZE YOUR STRESS TOMORROW!
(OR YOU CAN JUST WRITE OR DRAW SOMETHING SILLY DOWN BELOW AND GO TO BED SMILING.)
PLANS FOR TOMORROW/TO DO LIST:

"Success does not consist in never making mistakes but in never making the same one a second time."(1)   ~Bernard Shaw

Date ___ / ___ /20__

STRESSFUL MOMENTS:

_____

_____

_____

HAPPY MOMENTS:

_____

_____

_____

PLAN AHEAD TODAY TO MINIMIZE YOUR STRESS TOMORROW!
(OR YOU CAN JUST WRITE OR DRAW SOMETHING SILLY DOWN BELOW AND GO TO BED SMILING.)

PLANS FOR TOMORROW/TO DO LIST:

"Faith consists in believing when it is beyond the power of reason to believe."(5)

~Voltaire

Date ___/___/20__

STRESSFUL MOMENTS:

_____

_____

_____

HAPPY MOMENTS:

_____

_____

_____

PLAN AHEAD TODAY TO MINIMIZE YOUR STRESS TOMORROW!

(OR YOU CAN JUST WRITE OR DRAW SOMETHING SILLY DOWN BELOW AND GO TO BED SMILING.)

PLANS FOR TOMORROW/TO DO LIST:

"A pessimist is one who makes difficulties of his opportunities, and an optimist is one who makes opportunities of his difficulties."(10)

~Harry S. Truman

Date ___/___/20__

STRESSFUL MOMENTS:

_____

_____

_____

HAPPY MOMENTS:

_____

_____

_____

PLAN AHEAD TODAY TO MINIMIZE YOUR STRESS TOMORROW!

(OR YOU CAN JUST WRITE OR DRAW SOMETHING SILLY DOWN BELOW AND GO TO BED SMILING.)

PLANS FOR TOMORROW/TO DO LIST:

Motivation is critical! You have to find something you want to serve greater than yourself. Do it for your family, your community, society. The secret to living and being happy - is giving.

Date ___/___/20__

STRESSFUL MOMENTS:

_____

_____

_____

HAPPY MOMENTS:

_____

_____

_____

PLAN AHEAD TODAY TO MINIMIZE YOUR STRESS TOMORROW!
(OR YOU CAN JUST WRITE OR DRAW SOMETHING SILLY DOWN BELOW AND GO TO BED SMILING.)

PLANS FOR TOMORROW/TO DO LIST:

"Life is like riding a bicycle. To keep your balance you must keep moving."(10)

~Albert Einstein

Date ___/___/20__

STRESSFUL MOMENTS:

_____

_____

_____

HAPPY MOMENTS:

_____

_____

_____

PLAN AHEAD TODAY TO MINIMIZE YOUR STRESS TOMORROW!
(OR YOU CAN JUST WRITE OR DRAW SOMETHING SILLY DOWN BELOW AND GO TO BED SMILING.)

PLANS FOR TOMORROW/TO DO LIST:

Always try to focus on a present moment. When you are overwhelmed by negativity - just take a deep breath and concentrate on your surroundings. It will help you to relax and keep your mind away from destructive thoughts.

Date ___/___/20___

STRESSFUL MOMENTS:

_____

_____

_____

HAPPY MOMENTS:

_____

_____

_____

PLAN AHEAD TODAY TO MINIMIZE YOUR STRESS TOMORROW!
(OR YOU CAN JUST WRITE OR DRAW SOMETHING SILLY DOWN BELOW AND GO TO BED SMILING.)
PLANS FOR TOMORROW/TO DO LIST:

> "It is our attitude at the beginning of a difficult task which, more than anything else, will affect its successful outcome."(10)
>
> ~William James

Date ___/___/20___

STRESSFUL MOMENTS:

_____

_____

_____

HAPPY MOMENTS:

_____

_____

_____

PLAN AHEAD TODAY TO MINIMIZE YOUR STRESS TOMORROW!
(OR YOU CAN JUST WRITE OR DRAW SOMETHING SILLY DOWN BELOW AND GO TO BED SMILING.)
PLANS FOR TOMORROW/TO DO LIST:

"Trying to limit anybody about anything defies the Laws of the Universe. It cannot be done. You cannot control others, but you can control and create your own life."(10)   ~Abraham-Hicks

Date ___/___/20__

STRESSFUL MOMENTS:

_____

_____

_____

HAPPY MOMENTS:

_____

_____

_____

PLAN AHEAD TODAY TO MINIMIZE YOUR STRESS TOMORROW!

(OR YOU CAN JUST WRITE OR DRAW SOMETHING SILLY DOWN BELOW AND GO TO BED SMILING.)

PLANS FOR TOMORROW/TO DO LIST:

"Life must be lived and curiosity kept alive. One must never, for whatever reason, turn his back on life."(10)   ~Eleanor Roosevelt

Date ___/___/20__

STRESSFUL MOMENTS:

_____

_____

_____

HAPPY MOMENTS:

_____

_____

_____

PLAN AHEAD TODAY TO MINIMIZE YOUR STRESS TOMORROW!
(OR YOU CAN JUST WRITE OR DRAW SOMETHING SILLY DOWN BELOW AND GO TO BED SMILING.)
PLANS FOR TOMORROW/TO DO LIST:

"True friendship is a plant of slow growth and must undergo and withstand the shocks of adversity before it is entitled to the appellation."(10)

~George Washington

Date ___/___/20__

STRESSFUL MOMENTS:

_____

_____

_____

HAPPY MOMENTS:

_____

_____

_____

PLAN AHEAD TODAY TO MINIMIZE YOUR STRESS TOMORROW!

(OR YOU CAN JUST WRITE OR DRAW SOMETHING SILLY DOWN BELOW AND GO TO BED SMILING.)

PLANS FOR TOMORROW/TO DO LIST:

"Happiness does not lie in happiness, but in the achievement of it."(10)

~Dostoevsky

Date ___/___/20__

STRESSFUL MOMENTS:

_____

_____

_____

HAPPY MOMENTS:

_____

_____

_____

PLAN AHEAD TODAY TO MINIMIZE YOUR STRESS TOMORROW!
(OR YOU CAN JUST WRITE OR DRAW SOMETHING SILLY DOWN BELOW AND GO TO BED SMILING.)
PLANS FOR TOMORROW/TO DO LIST:

"It is understanding that gives us an ability to have peace. When we understand the other fellow's viewpoint, and he understands ours, then we can sit down and work out our differences."(10)

~Harry Truman

Date ___/___/20__

STRESSFUL MOMENTS:

_____

_____

_____

HAPPY MOMENTS:

_____

_____

_____

PLAN AHEAD TODAY TO MINIMIZE YOUR STRESS TOMORROW!

(OR YOU CAN JUST WRITE OR DRAW SOMETHING SILLY DOWN BELOW AND GO TO BED SMILING.)

PLANS FOR TOMORROW/TO DO LIST:

"We are shaped by our thoughts; we become what we think. When the mind is pure, joy follows like a shadow that never leaves."(10)
~The Buddha

Date ___/___/20__

STRESSFUL MOMENTS:

_____

_____

_____

HAPPY MOMENTS:

_____

_____

_____

PLAN AHEAD TODAY TO MINIMIZE YOUR STRESS TOMORROW!
(OR YOU CAN JUST WRITE OR DRAW SOMETHING SILLY DOWN BELOW AND GO TO BED SMILING.)
PLANS FOR TOMORROW/TO DO LIST:

"For every minute you remain angry, you give up sixty seconds of peace of mind."(10)

~R. W. Emerson

Date ___/___/20__

STRESSFUL MOMENTS:

_____

_____

_____

HAPPY MOMENTS:

_____

_____

_____

PLAN AHEAD TODAY TO MINIMIZE YOUR STRESS TOMORROW!
(OR YOU CAN JUST WRITE OR DRAW SOMETHING SILLY DOWN BELOW AND GO TO BED SMILING.)
PLANS FOR TOMORROW/TO DO LIST:

"I believe that every human mind feels pleasure in doing good to another."(10)

~Thomas Jefferson

Date ___/___/20__

STRESSFUL MOMENTS:

_____

_____

_____

HAPPY MOMENTS:

_____

_____

_____

PLAN AHEAD TODAY TO MINIMIZE YOUR STRESS TOMORROW!
(OR YOU CAN JUST WRITE OR DRAW SOMETHING SILLY DOWN BELOW AND GO TO BED SMILING.)

PLANS FOR TOMORROW/TO DO LIST:

> "A life spent making mistakes is not only more honorable but more useful than a life spent doing nothing."(1)
> ~Bernard Shaw

Date ___/___/20___

STRESSFUL MOMENTS:

_____

_____

_____

HAPPY MOMENTS:

_____

_____

_____

PLAN AHEAD TODAY TO MINIMIZE YOUR STRESS TOMORROW!
(OR YOU CAN JUST WRITE OR DRAW SOMETHING SILLY DOWN BELOW AND GO TO BED SMILING.)
PLANS FOR TOMORROW/TO DO LIST:

"Now and then it's good to pause in our pursuit of happiness and just be happy."(10)

~G. Apollinaire

Date ___/___/20__

STRESSFUL MOMENTS:

_____

_____

_____

HAPPY MOMENTS:

_____

_____

_____

PLAN AHEAD TODAY TO MINIMIZE YOUR STRESS TOMORROW!

(OR YOU CAN JUST WRITE OR DRAW SOMETHING SILLY DOWN BELOW AND GO TO BED SMILING.)

PLANS FOR TOMORROW/TO DO LIST:

"It takes great wit and interest and energy to be happy. The pursuit of happiness is a great activity. One must be open and alive. It is the greatest feat man has to accomplish."[10]

~R. Herrick

Date ___/___/20__

STRESSFUL MOMENTS:

_____

_____

_____

HAPPY MOMENTS:

_____

_____

_____

PLAN AHEAD TODAY TO MINIMIZE YOUR STRESS TOMORROW!
(OR YOU CAN JUST WRITE OR DRAW SOMETHING SILLY DOWN BELOW AND GO TO BED SMILING.)

PLANS FOR TOMORROW/TO DO LIST:

Positive thoughts have the power to shape you into a positive person.

Date ___ / ___ /20__

STRESSFUL MOMENTS:

_____

_____

_____

HAPPY MOMENTS:

_____

_____

_____

PLAN AHEAD TODAY TO MINIMIZE YOUR STRESS TOMORROW!
(OR YOU CAN JUST WRITE OR DRAW SOMETHING SILLY DOWN BELOW AND GO TO BED SMILING.)
PLANS FOR TOMORROW/TO DO LIST:

"Be happy for this moment. This moment is your life."(10)

~Omar Khayyam

Date ___/___/20__

STRESSFUL MOMENTS:

_____

_____

_____

HAPPY MOMENTS:

_____

_____

_____

PLAN AHEAD TODAY TO MINIMIZE YOUR STRESS TOMORROW!

(OR YOU CAN JUST WRITE OR DRAW SOMETHING SILLY DOWN BELOW AND GO TO BED SMILING.)

PLANS FOR TOMORROW/TO DO LIST:

"Watch your thoughts, for they become words. Watch your words, for they become actions. Watch your actions, for they become habits. Watch your habits, for they become the character. Watch your character, for it becomes your destiny."(5)   ~unknown

Date ___/___/20__

STRESSFUL MOMENTS:

_____

_____

_____

HAPPY MOMENTS:

_____

_____

_____

PLAN AHEAD TODAY TO MINIMIZE YOUR STRESS TOMORROW!
(OR YOU CAN JUST WRITE OR DRAW SOMETHING SILLY DOWN BELOW AND GO TO BED SMILING.)
PLANS FOR TOMORROW/TO DO LIST:

"Your worst enemy cannot harm you as much as your own unguarded thoughts."(10)

Date ___/___/20__

STRESSFUL MOMENTS:

_____

_____

_____

HAPPY MOMENTS:

_____

_____

_____

PLAN AHEAD TODAY TO MINIMIZE YOUR STRESS TOMORROW!
(OR YOU CAN JUST WRITE OR DRAW SOMETHING SILLY DOWN BELOW AND GO TO BED SMILING.)
PLANS FOR TOMORROW/TO DO LIST:

"The happiness of one's own heart alone cannot satisfy the soul; one must try to include, as necessary to one's own happiness, the happiness of others."(10)
~Paramahansa Yogananda

Date ___/___/20__

STRESSFUL MOMENTS:

_____

_____

_____

HAPPY MOMENTS:

_____

_____

_____

PLAN AHEAD TODAY TO MINIMIZE YOUR STRESS TOMORROW!
(OR YOU CAN JUST WRITE OR DRAW SOMETHING SILLY DOWN BELOW AND GO TO BED SMILING.)
PLANS FOR TOMORROW/TO DO LIST:

"To enjoy good health, to bring true happiness to one's family, to bring peace to all, one must first discipline and control one's own mind. If a man can control his mind, he can find the way to Enlightenment, and all wisdom and virtue will naturally come to him."(10)

~Buddha

Date ___/___/20__

STRESSFUL MOMENTS:

_____

_____

_____

HAPPY MOMENTS:

_____

_____

_____

PLAN AHEAD TODAY TO MINIMIZE YOUR STRESS TOMORROW!
(OR YOU CAN JUST WRITE OR DRAW SOMETHING SILLY DOWN BELOW AND GO TO BED SMILING.)
PLANS FOR TOMORROW/TO DO LIST:

After switching to positive thinking, the next step is trying to maintain a positive state of mind. Identify which power emotions give you happiness. Cultivate them and keep them alive.

Date ___/___/20__

STRESSFUL MOMENTS:

_____

_____

_____

HAPPY MOMENTS:

_____

_____

_____

PLAN AHEAD TODAY TO MINIMIZE YOUR STRESS TOMORROW!
(OR YOU CAN JUST WRITE OR DRAW SOMETHING SILLY DOWN BELOW AND GO TO BED SMILING.)
PLANS FOR TOMORROW/TO DO LIST:

"There is a magnet in your heart that will attract true friends. That magnet is unselfishness, thinking of others first; when you learn to live for others, they will live for you."(10)   ~Paramahansa Yogananda

Date ___ / ___ /20___

STRESSFUL MOMENTS:

_____

_____

_____

HAPPY MOMENTS:

_____

_____

_____

PLAN AHEAD TODAY TO MINIMIZE YOUR STRESS TOMORROW!
(OR YOU CAN JUST WRITE OR DRAW SOMETHING SILLY DOWN BELOW AND GO TO BED SMILING.)
PLANS FOR TOMORROW/TO DO LIST:

"Happiness is when what you think, what you say, and what you do are in harmony."(10)

~M. Gandhi

Date ___/___/20__

STRESSFUL MOMENTS:

_____

_____

_____

HAPPY MOMENTS:

_____

_____

_____

PLAN AHEAD TODAY TO MINIMIZE YOUR STRESS TOMORROW!

(OR YOU CAN JUST WRITE OR DRAW SOMETHING SILLY DOWN BELOW AND GO TO BED SMILING.)

PLANS FOR TOMORROW/TO DO LIST:

"Start every day off with a smile and get it over with."(5)´ ~W.C. Fields

Date ___/___/20__

STRESSFUL MOMENTS:

_____

_____

_____

HAPPY MOMENTS:

_____

_____

_____

PLAN AHEAD TODAY TO MINIMIZE YOUR STRESS TOMORROW!

(OR YOU CAN JUST WRITE OR DRAW SOMETHING SILLY DOWN BELOW AND GO TO BED SMILING.)

PLANS FOR TOMORROW/TO DO LIST:

Optimism is one of the most essential qualities that will lead you to happiness and success!

Date ___/___/20__

STRESSFUL MOMENTS:

_____

_____

_____

HAPPY MOMENTS:

_____

_____

_____

PLAN AHEAD TODAY TO MINIMIZE YOUR STRESS TOMORROW!

(OR YOU CAN JUST WRITE OR DRAW SOMETHING SILLY DOWN BELOW AND GO TO BED SMILING.)

PLANS FOR TOMORROW/TO DO LIST:

> "True happiness arises, in the first place, from the enjoyment of one's self, and in the next, from the friendship and conversation of a few select companions."(10)
>
> ~Joseph Addison

Date ___/___/20__

STRESSFUL MOMENTS:

_____

_____

_____

HAPPY MOMENTS:

_____

_____

_____

PLAN AHEAD TODAY TO MINIMIZE YOUR STRESS TOMORROW!

(OR YOU CAN JUST WRITE OR DRAW SOMETHING SILLY DOWN BELOW AND GO TO BED SMILING.)

PLANS FOR TOMORROW/TO DO LIST:

Don't waste even a single minute of your life. WE ONLY LIVE ONCE!

Date ___/___/20__

STRESSFUL MOMENTS:

_____

_____

_____

HAPPY MOMENTS:

_____

_____

_____

PLAN AHEAD TODAY TO MINIMIZE YOUR STRESS TOMORROW!
(OR YOU CAN JUST WRITE OR DRAW SOMETHING SILLY DOWN BELOW AND GO TO BED SMILING.)
PLANS FOR TOMORROW/TO DO LIST:

"Three grand essentials to happiness in this life are something to do, something to love, and something to hope for."(10) ~Joseph Addison

Date ___/___/20__

STRESSFUL MOMENTS:

_____

_____

_____

HAPPY MOMENTS:

_____

_____

_____

PLAN AHEAD TODAY TO MINIMIZE YOUR STRESS TOMORROW!
(OR YOU CAN JUST WRITE OR DRAW SOMETHING SILLY DOWN BELOW AND GO TO BED SMILING.)
PLANS FOR TOMORROW/TO DO LIST:

"Half the world is composed of people who have something to say and can't, and the other half who have nothing to say and keep on saying it."(5)
~R. Frost

Date ___/___/20__

STRESSFUL MOMENTS:

_____

_____

_____

HAPPY MOMENTS:

_____

_____

_____

PLAN AHEAD TODAY TO MINIMIZE YOUR STRESS TOMORROW!
(OR YOU CAN JUST WRITE OR DRAW SOMETHING SILLY DOWN BELOW AND GO TO BED SMILING.)
PLANS FOR TOMORROW/TO DO LIST:

"The happiness of your life depends upon the quality of your thoughts: therefore, guard accordingly."(10)   ~Marcus Aurelius

Date ___/___/20__

STRESSFUL MOMENTS:

_____

_____

_____

HAPPY MOMENTS:

_____

_____

_____

PLAN AHEAD TODAY TO MINIMIZE YOUR STRESS TOMORROW!
(OR YOU CAN JUST WRITE OR DRAW SOMETHING SILLY DOWN BELOW AND GO TO BED SMILING.)
PLANS FOR TOMORROW/TO DO LIST:

"We are what we repeatedly do. Excellence, then is not an act, but a habit."(5)

~Aristotle

Date ___/___/20__

STRESSFUL MOMENTS:

_____

_____

_____

HAPPY MOMENTS:

_____

_____

_____

PLAN AHEAD TODAY TO MINIMIZE YOUR STRESS TOMORROW!
(OR YOU CAN JUST WRITE OR DRAW SOMETHING SILLY DOWN BELOW AND GO TO BED SMILING.)
PLANS FOR TOMORROW/TO DO LIST:

"Worrying doesn't take away tomorrow's trouble; it takes away today's peace."(10)

Date ___/___/20__

STRESSFUL MOMENTS:

_____

_____

_____

HAPPY MOMENTS:

_____

_____

_____

PLAN AHEAD TODAY TO MINIMIZE YOUR STRESS TOMORROW!
(OR YOU CAN JUST WRITE OR DRAW SOMETHING SILLY DOWN BELOW AND GO TO BED SMILING.)
PLANS FOR TOMORROW/TO DO LIST:

"When you have a dozen reasons to smile, don't let one reason make you frown."(10)

~unknown

Date ___ / ___ /20__

STRESSFUL MOMENTS:

_____

_____

_____

HAPPY MOMENTS:

_____

_____

_____

PLAN AHEAD TODAY TO MINIMIZE YOUR STRESS TOMORROW!
(OR YOU CAN JUST WRITE OR DRAW SOMETHING SILLY DOWN BELOW AND GO TO BED SMILING.)
PLANS FOR TOMORROW/TO DO LIST:

"When you arise in the morning, think of what a precious privilege it is to be alive - to breathe, to think, to enjoy, to love."(10)

~Marcus Aurelius

Date ___/___/20__

STRESSFUL MOMENTS:

_____

_____

_____

HAPPY MOMENTS:

_____

_____

_____

PLAN AHEAD TODAY TO MINIMIZE YOUR STRESS TOMORROW!
(OR YOU CAN JUST WRITE OR DRAW SOMETHING SILLY DOWN BELOW AND GO TO BED SMILING.)
PLANS FOR TOMORROW/TO DO LIST:

"Very little is needed to make a happy life; it is all within yourself, in your way of thinking."(10)

~Marcus Aurelius

Date ___/___/20__

STRESSFUL MOMENTS:

_____

_____

_____

HAPPY MOMENTS:

_____

_____

_____

PLAN AHEAD TODAY TO MINIMIZE YOUR STRESS TOMORROW!

(OR YOU CAN JUST WRITE OR DRAW SOMETHING SILLY DOWN BELOW AND GO TO BED SMILING.)

PLANS FOR TOMORROW/TO DO LIST:

> "Anger is an acid that can do more harm to the vessel in which it is stored than to anything on which it is poured."(10)   ~Mark Twain

Date ___/___/20___

STRESSFUL MOMENTS:

_____

_____

_____

HAPPY MOMENTS:

_____

_____

_____

PLAN AHEAD TODAY TO MINIMIZE YOUR STRESS TOMORROW!
(OR YOU CAN JUST WRITE OR DRAW SOMETHING SILLY DOWN BELOW AND GO TO BED SMILING.)
PLANS FOR TOMORROW/TO DO LIST:

The happiness of your life entirely depends on the positivity of your thoughts and attitude. Trust your gut feeling. Walk away from negative environments and negative people.

Date ___ / ___ /20__

STRESSFUL MOMENTS:

_____

_____

_____

HAPPY MOMENTS:

_____

_____

_____

PLAN AHEAD TODAY TO MINIMIZE YOUR STRESS TOMORROW!
(OR YOU CAN JUST WRITE OR DRAW SOMETHING SILLY DOWN BELOW AND GO TO BED SMILING.)
PLANS FOR TOMORROW/TO DO LIST:

> "Life is short; live it. Love is rare; grab it. Anger is bad; dump it. Fear is awful; face it. Memories are sweet; cherish it."(10)   ~unknown

Date ___/___/20__

STRESSFUL MOMENTS:

_____

_____

_____

HAPPY MOMENTS:

_____

_____

_____

PLAN AHEAD TODAY TO MINIMIZE YOUR STRESS TOMORROW!
(OR YOU CAN JUST WRITE OR DRAW SOMETHING SILLY DOWN BELOW AND GO TO BED SMILING.)
PLANS FOR TOMORROW/TO DO LIST:

> "The right word may be effective, but no word was ever as effective as a rightly timed pause."(10)
>
> ~Mark Twain

Date ___/___/20__

STRESSFUL MOMENTS:

_____

_____

_____

HAPPY MOMENTS:

_____

_____

_____

PLAN AHEAD TODAY TO MINIMIZE YOUR STRESS TOMORROW!

(OR YOU CAN JUST WRITE OR DRAW SOMETHING SILLY DOWN BELOW AND GO TO BED SMILING.)

PLANS FOR TOMORROW/TO DO LIST:

"Actions are the seed of fate; deeds grow into destiny."(10)

~Harry S. Truman

Date ___/___/20__

STRESSFUL MOMENTS:

_____

_____

_____

HAPPY MOMENTS:

_____

_____

_____

PLAN AHEAD TODAY TO MINIMIZE YOUR STRESS TOMORROW!

(OR YOU CAN JUST WRITE OR DRAW SOMETHING SILLY DOWN BELOW AND GO TO BED SMILING.)

PLANS FOR TOMORROW/TO DO LIST:

"When people hurt you over and over, think of them like sandpaper. They may scratch and hurt a bit, but in the end, you end up polished, and they end up useless."(10)   ~unknown

Date ___/___/20__

STRESSFUL MOMENTS:

_____

_____

_____

HAPPY MOMENTS:

_____

_____

_____

PLAN AHEAD TODAY TO MINIMIZE YOUR STRESS TOMORROW!
(OR YOU CAN JUST WRITE OR DRAW SOMETHING SILLY DOWN BELOW AND GO TO BED SMILING.)
PLANS FOR TOMORROW/TO DO LIST:

Don't feel sorry for yourself - such a waste of time! Instead, work toward your success and happiness.

Date ___/___/20__

STRESSFUL MOMENTS:

_____

_____

_____

HAPPY MOMENTS:

_____

_____

_____

PLAN AHEAD TODAY TO MINIMIZE YOUR STRESS TOMORROW!
(OR YOU CAN JUST WRITE OR DRAW SOMETHING SILLY DOWN BELOW AND GO TO BED SMILING.)

PLANS FOR TOMORROW/TO DO LIST:

"Our greatest glory is not in never falling but in rising every time we fall."(10)

~Confucius

Date ___/___/20__

STRESSFUL MOMENTS:

_____

_____

_____

HAPPY MOMENTS:

_____

_____

_____

PLAN AHEAD TODAY TO MINIMIZE YOUR STRESS TOMORROW!

(OR YOU CAN JUST WRITE OR DRAW SOMETHING SILLY DOWN BELOW AND GO TO BED SMILING.)

PLANS FOR TOMORROW/TO DO LIST:

> "Age is an issue of mind over matter. If you don't mind, it's doesn't matter."(10)
>
> ~Mark Twain

Date ___/___/20__

STRESSFUL MOMENTS:

_____

_____

_____

HAPPY MOMENTS:

_____

_____

_____

PLAN AHEAD TODAY TO MINIMIZE YOUR STRESS TOMORROW!

(OR YOU CAN JUST WRITE OR DRAW SOMETHING SILLY DOWN BELOW AND GO TO BED SMILING.)

PLANS FOR TOMORROW/TO DO LIST:

"You will not be punished FOR your anger; you will be punished BY your anger."(5)

Date ___/___/20__

STRESSFUL MOMENTS:

_____

_____

_____

HAPPY MOMENTS:

_____

_____

_____

PLAN AHEAD TODAY TO MINIMIZE YOUR STRESS TOMORROW!
(OR YOU CAN JUST WRITE OR DRAW SOMETHING SILLY DOWN BELOW AND GO TO BED SMILING.)
PLANS FOR TOMORROW/TO DO LIST:

"Nothing can stop the man with the right mental attitude from achieving his goal; nothing on earth can help the man with the wrong mental attitude."(5)

~Thomas Jefferson

Date ___/___/20__

STRESSFUL MOMENTS:

_____

_____

_____

HAPPY MOMENTS:

_____

_____

_____

PLAN AHEAD TODAY TO MINIMIZE YOUR STRESS TOMORROW!

(OR YOU CAN JUST WRITE OR DRAW SOMETHING SILLY DOWN BELOW AND GO TO BED SMILING.)

PLANS FOR TOMORROW/TO DO LIST:

IMAGINE, BELIEVE, ACHIEVE!

Date ___/___/20__

STRESSFUL MOMENTS:

_____

_____

_____

HAPPY MOMENTS:

_____

_____

_____

PLAN AHEAD TODAY TO MINIMIZE YOUR STRESS TOMORROW!
(OR YOU CAN JUST WRITE OR DRAW SOMETHING SILLY DOWN BELOW AND GO TO BED SMILING.)
PLANS FOR TOMORROW/TO DO LIST:

"**There is only one way to happiness, and that is to cease worrying about things which are beyond the power of our will.**"(10) ~Epictetus

Date ___/___/20__

STRESSFUL MOMENTS:

_____

_____

_____

HAPPY MOMENTS:

_____

_____

_____

PLAN AHEAD TODAY TO MINIMIZE YOUR STRESS TOMORROW!
(OR YOU CAN JUST WRITE OR DRAW SOMETHING SILLY DOWN BELOW AND GO TO BED SMILING.)
PLANS FOR TOMORROW/TO DO LIST:

"**Many people think that patience is a sign of weakness. I think this is a mistake. It is anger that is a sign of weakness, whereas patience is a sign of strength.**"(10)

~Dalai Lama

Date ___/___/20__

STRESSFUL MOMENTS:

_____

_____

_____

HAPPY MOMENTS:

_____

_____

_____

PLAN AHEAD TODAY TO MINIMIZE YOUR STRESS TOMORROW!

(OR YOU CAN JUST WRITE OR DRAW SOMETHING SILLY DOWN BELOW AND GO TO BED SMILING.)

PLANS FOR TOMORROW/TO DO LIST:

You always need to ask yourself if what you are doing today is getting you closer to where you want to be tomorrow.

Date ___/___/20___

STRESSFUL MOMENTS:

_____

_____

_____

HAPPY MOMENTS:

_____

_____

_____

PLAN AHEAD TODAY TO MINIMIZE YOUR STRESS TOMORROW!

(OR YOU CAN JUST WRITE OR DRAW SOMETHING SILLY DOWN BELOW AND GO TO BED SMILING.)

PLANS FOR TOMORROW/TO DO LIST:

"Failure is the opportunity to begin again more intelligently."(2)

~Henry Ford

Date ___/___/20__

STRESSFUL MOMENTS:

_____

_____

_____

HAPPY MOMENTS:

_____

_____

_____

PLAN AHEAD TODAY TO MINIMIZE YOUR STRESS TOMORROW!
(OR YOU CAN JUST WRITE OR DRAW SOMETHING SILLY DOWN BELOW AND GO TO BED SMILING.)
PLANS FOR TOMORROW/TO DO LIST:

> "Worry is the total waste of time. It doesn't change anything. All it does is steal your joy and keep you very busy doing nothing."(10)
>
> -Anonymous

Date ___/___/20__

STRESSFUL MOMENTS:

_____

_____

_____

HAPPY MOMENTS:

_____

_____

_____

PLAN AHEAD TODAY TO MINIMIZE YOUR STRESS TOMORROW!

(OR YOU CAN JUST WRITE OR DRAW SOMETHING SILLY DOWN BELOW AND GO TO BED SMILING.)

PLANS FOR TOMORROW/TO DO LIST:

"The key is to keep company only with people who uplift you, whose presence calls forth your best."(5)   ~Epictetus

Date ___/___/20__

STRESSFUL MOMENTS:

_____

_____

_____

HAPPY MOMENTS:

_____

_____

_____

PLAN AHEAD TODAY TO MINIMIZE YOUR STRESS TOMORROW!
(OR YOU CAN JUST WRITE OR DRAW SOMETHING SILLY DOWN BELOW AND GO TO BED SMILING.)
PLANS FOR TOMORROW/TO DO LIST:

> "It is during our darkest moments that we must focus to see the light."(5)
> ~Aristotle

Date ___/___/20__

STRESSFUL MOMENTS:

_____

_____

_____

HAPPY MOMENTS:

_____

_____

_____

PLAN AHEAD TODAY TO MINIMIZE YOUR STRESS TOMORROW!
(OR YOU CAN JUST WRITE OR DRAW SOMETHING SILLY DOWN BELOW AND GO TO BED SMILING.)

PLANS FOR TOMORROW/TO DO LIST:

> **"Peace is not the absence of conflict; it is the ability to handle conflict by peaceful means."**(3)
>
> ~Ronald Reagan

Date ___/___/20__

STRESSFUL MOMENTS:

_____

_____

_____

HAPPY MOMENTS:

_____

_____

_____

PLAN AHEAD TODAY TO MINIMIZE YOUR STRESS TOMORROW!

(OR YOU CAN JUST WRITE OR DRAW SOMETHING SILLY DOWN BELOW AND GO TO BED SMILING.)

PLANS FOR TOMORROW/TO DO LIST:

"Never put the key to your happiness in someone else's pocket."(10)

.   ~unknown

Date ___/___/20__

STRESSFUL MOMENTS:

_____

_____

_____

HAPPY MOMENTS:

_____

_____

_____

PLAN AHEAD TODAY TO MINIMIZE YOUR STRESS TOMORROW!
(OR YOU CAN JUST WRITE OR DRAW SOMETHING SILLY DOWN BELOW AND GO TO BED SMILING.)
PLANS FOR TOMORROW/TO DO LIST:

~Will Rogers

Date ___/___/20__

STRESSFUL MOMENTS:

_____

_____

_____

HAPPY MOMENTS:

_____

_____

_____

PLAN AHEAD TODAY TO MINIMIZE YOUR STRESS TOMORROW!

(OR YOU CAN JUST WRITE OR DRAW SOMETHING SILLY DOWN BELOW AND GO TO BED SMILING.)

PLANS FOR TOMORROW/TO DO LIST:

"Believe you can and you're halfway there."(5)   ~Theodore Roosevelt

Date ___/___/20__

STRESSFUL MOMENTS:

_____

_____

_____

HAPPY MOMENTS:

_____

_____

_____

PLAN AHEAD TODAY TO MINIMIZE YOUR STRESS TOMORROW!
(OR YOU CAN JUST WRITE OR DRAW SOMETHING SILLY DOWN BELOW AND GO TO BED SMILING.)
PLANS FOR TOMORROW/TO DO LIST:

"Strong minds discuss ideas, average minds discuss events, weak minds discuss people."(10)   ~Socrates

Date ___ / ___ /20 __

STRESSFUL MOMENTS:

_____

_____

_____

HAPPY MOMENTS:

_____

_____

_____

PLAN AHEAD TODAY TO MINIMIZE YOUR STRESS TOMORROW!
(OR YOU CAN JUST WRITE OR DRAW SOMETHING SILLY DOWN BELOW AND GO TO BED SMILING.)
PLANS FOR TOMORROW/TO DO LIST:

"If you believe in what you are doing, then let nothing hold you up in your work. Much of the best work of the world has been done against seeming impossibilities. The thing is to get the work done."(5)

~Dale Carnegie

Date ___/___/20__

STRESSFUL MOMENTS:

_____

_____

_____

HAPPY MOMENTS:

_____

_____

_____

PLAN AHEAD TODAY TO MINIMIZE YOUR STRESS TOMORROW!
(OR YOU CAN JUST WRITE OR DRAW SOMETHING SILLY DOWN BELOW AND GO TO BED SMILING.)
PLANS FOR TOMORROW/TO DO LIST:

"If you want to be successful, it's just this simple. Know what you are doing. Love what you are doing. And believe in what you are doing."(5)

~Will Rogers

Date ___/___/20__

STRESSFUL MOMENTS:

_____

_____

_____

HAPPY MOMENTS:

_____

_____

_____

PLAN AHEAD TODAY TO MINIMIZE YOUR STRESS TOMORROW!

(OR YOU CAN JUST WRITE OR DRAW SOMETHING SILLY DOWN BELOW AND GO TO BED SMILING.)

PLANS FOR TOMORROW/TO DO LIST:

"Be slow to fall into friendship, but when you are in, continue firm and constant."(5)

~Socrates

Date ___/___/20__

STRESSFUL MOMENTS:

_____

_____

_____

HAPPY MOMENTS:

_____

_____

_____

PLAN AHEAD TODAY TO MINIMIZE YOUR STRESS TOMORROW!

(OR YOU CAN JUST WRITE OR DRAW SOMETHING SILLY DOWN BELOW AND GO TO BED SMILING.)

PLANS FOR TOMORROW/TO DO LIST:

> **"Remember, happiness doesn't depend upon who you are or what you have; it depends solely on what you think."**(10)   ~Dale Carnegie

Date ___/___/20__

STRESSFUL MOMENTS:

_____

_____

_____

HAPPY MOMENTS:

_____

_____

_____

PLAN AHEAD TODAY TO MINIMIZE YOUR STRESS TOMORROW!
(OR YOU CAN JUST WRITE OR DRAW SOMETHING SILLY DOWN BELOW AND GO TO BED SMILING.)

PLANS FOR TOMORROW/TO DO LIST:

> **"Develop success from failures. Discouragement and failure are two of the surest stepping stones to success."** (10)
>
> ~Dale Carnegie

Date ___/___/20___

STRESSFUL MOMENTS:

_____

_____

_____

HAPPY MOMENTS:

_____

_____

_____

PLAN AHEAD TODAY TO MINIMIZE YOUR STRESS TOMORROW!
(OR YOU CAN JUST WRITE OR DRAW SOMETHING SILLY DOWN BELOW AND GO TO BED SMILING.)
PLANS FOR TOMORROW/TO DO LIST:

"Sometimes you put walls up not to keep people out, but to see who cares enough to break them down."(10)   ~Socrates

Date ___ / ___ /20__

STRESSFUL MOMENTS:

_____

_____

_____

HAPPY MOMENTS:

_____

_____

_____

PLAN AHEAD TODAY TO MINIMIZE YOUR STRESS TOMORROW!
(OR YOU CAN JUST WRITE OR DRAW SOMETHING SILLY DOWN BELOW AND GO TO BED SMILING.)
PLANS FOR TOMORROW/TO DO LIST:

"The secret of happiness, you see, is not found in seeking more, but in developing the capacity to enjoy less."(10)   ~Socrates

Date ___/___/20___

STRESSFUL MOMENTS:

_____

_____

_____

HAPPY MOMENTS:

_____

_____

_____

PLAN AHEAD TODAY TO MINIMIZE YOUR STRESS TOMORROW!

(OR YOU CAN JUST WRITE OR DRAW SOMETHING SILLY DOWN BELOW AND GO TO BED SMILING.)

PLANS FOR TOMORROW/TO DO LIST:

"Do not do to others what angers you if done to you by others."(10)

~Socrates

Date ___/___/20__

STRESSFUL MOMENTS:

_____

_____

_____

HAPPY MOMENTS:

_____

_____

_____

PLAN AHEAD TODAY TO MINIMIZE YOUR STRESS TOMORROW!
(OR YOU CAN JUST WRITE OR DRAW SOMETHING SILLY DOWN BELOW AND GO TO BED SMILING.)
PLANS FOR TOMORROW/TO DO LIST:

"Darkness cannot drive out darkness; only light can do that. Hate cannot drive out hate; only love can do that."(5)   ~Martin Luther King Jr

Date ___/___/20__

STRESSFUL MOMENTS:

_____

_____

_____

HAPPY MOMENTS:

_____

_____

_____

PLAN AHEAD TODAY TO MINIMIZE YOUR STRESS TOMORROW!

(OR YOU CAN JUST WRITE OR DRAW SOMETHING SILLY DOWN BELOW AND GO TO BED SMILING.)

PLANS FOR TOMORROW/TO DO LIST:

"Don't waste your love on somebody who doesn't value it."(5)

~William Shakespeare

Date ___ / ___ /20__

STRESSFUL MOMENTS:

_____

_____

_____

HAPPY MOMENTS:

_____

_____

_____

PLAN AHEAD TODAY TO MINIMIZE YOUR STRESS TOMORROW!

(OR YOU CAN JUST WRITE OR DRAW SOMETHING SILLY DOWN BELOW AND GO TO BED SMILING.)

PLANS FOR TOMORROW/TO DO LIST:

"Take a chance! All life is a chance. The man who goes farthest is generally the one who is willing to do and dare."(10)   ~Dale Carnegie

Date ___/___/20__

STRESSFUL MOMENTS:

_____

_____

_____

HAPPY MOMENTS:

_____

_____

_____

PLAN AHEAD TODAY TO MINIMIZE YOUR STRESS TOMORROW!

(OR YOU CAN JUST WRITE OR DRAW SOMETHING SILLY DOWN BELOW AND GO TO BED SMILING.)

PLANS FOR TOMORROW/TO DO LIST:

"Today is the life - the only life you are sure of. Make the most of today. Get interested in something. Shake yourself awake. Develop a hobby. Let the winds of enthusiasm sweep through you."(10)

~Dale Carnegie

Date ___/___/20__

STRESSFUL MOMENTS:

_____

_____

_____

HAPPY MOMENTS:

_____

_____

_____

PLAN AHEAD TODAY TO MINIMIZE YOUR STRESS TOMORROW!
(OR YOU CAN JUST WRITE OR DRAW SOMETHING SILLY DOWN BELOW AND GO TO BED SMILING.)
PLANS FOR TOMORROW/TO DO LIST:

"We are shaped by our thoughts; we become what we think. When the mind is pure, joy follows like a shadow that never leaves."(10)

~Buddha

Date ___/___/20___

STRESSFUL MOMENTS:

_____
_____

_____
_____

_____
_____

HAPPY MOMENTS:

_____
_____

_____
_____

_____
_____

PLAN AHEAD TODAY TO MINIMIZE YOUR STRESS TOMORROW!
(OR YOU CAN JUST WRITE OR DRAW SOMETHING SILLY DOWN BELOW AND GO TO BED SMILING.)
PLANS FOR TOMORROW/TO DO LIST:

"Let your smile change the world, but don't let the world change your smile."(10)

~unknown

Date ___/___/20__

STRESSFUL MOMENTS:

_____

_____

_____

HAPPY MOMENTS:

_____

_____

_____

PLAN AHEAD TODAY TO MINIMIZE YOUR STRESS TOMORROW!
(OR YOU CAN JUST WRITE OR DRAW SOMETHING SILLY DOWN BELOW AND GO TO BED SMILING.)
PLANS FOR TOMORROW/TO DO LIST:

"Holding on to anger is like grasping a hot coal with the intent of throwing it at someone else; you are the one who gets burned."(10)

~Buddha

Date ___/___/20___

STRESSFUL MOMENTS:

_____

_____

_____

HAPPY MOMENTS:

_____

_____

_____

PLAN AHEAD TODAY TO MINIMIZE YOUR STRESS TOMORROW!

(OR YOU CAN JUST WRITE OR DRAW SOMETHING SILLY DOWN BELOW AND GO TO BED SMILING.)

PLANS FOR TOMORROW/TO DO LIST:

"Success is getting what you want. Happiness is wanting what you get."(10)   ~unknown

Date ___/___/20__

STRESSFUL MOMENTS:

_____

_____

_____

HAPPY MOMENTS:

_____

_____

_____

PLAN AHEAD TODAY TO MINIMIZE YOUR STRESS TOMORROW!
(OR YOU CAN JUST WRITE OR DRAW SOMETHING SILLY DOWN BELOW AND GO TO BED SMILING.)
PLANS FOR TOMORROW/TO DO LIST:

"One of the most tragic things I know about human nature is that all of us tend to put off living. We are all dreaming of some magical rose garden over the horizon instead of enjoying the roses that are blooming outside our windows today."(10)   ~Dale Carnegie

Date ___/___/20__

STRESSFUL MOMENTS:

_____

_____

_____

HAPPY MOMENTS:

_____

_____

_____

PLAN AHEAD TODAY TO MINIMIZE YOUR STRESS TOMORROW!
(OR YOU CAN JUST WRITE OR DRAW SOMETHING SILLY DOWN BELOW AND GO TO BED SMILING.)

PLANS FOR TOMORROW/TO DO LIST:

"Everything in life is temporary. So if things are going good, enjoy it because it won't last forever. And if things are going bad, don't worry. It can't last forever either."(10)   ~unknown

Date ___/___/20__

STRESSFUL MOMENTS:

_____

_____

_____

HAPPY MOMENTS:

_____

_____

_____

PLAN AHEAD TODAY TO MINIMIZE YOUR STRESS TOMORROW!
(OR YOU CAN JUST WRITE OR DRAW SOMETHING SILLY DOWN BELOW AND GO TO BED SMILING.)
PLANS FOR TOMORROW/TO DO LIST:

"Sometimes the best thing you can do is not think, not wonder, not imagine, not obsess. Just breathe and have faith that everything will work out for the best."(10)

~unknown

Date ___/___/20__

STRESSFUL MOMENTS:

_____

_____

_____

HAPPY MOMENTS:

_____

_____

_____

PLAN AHEAD TODAY TO MINIMIZE YOUR STRESS TOMORROW!

(OR YOU CAN JUST WRITE OR DRAW SOMETHING SILLY DOWN BELOW AND GO TO BED SMILING.)

PLANS FOR TOMORROW/TO DO LIST:

> **"Happiness doesn't depend on any external conditions; it is governed by our mental attitude."**(10)
>
> ~Dale Carnegie

Date ___/___/20__

STRESSFUL MOMENTS:

_____

_____

_____

HAPPY MOMENTS:

_____

_____

_____

PLAN AHEAD TODAY TO MINIMIZE YOUR STRESS TOMORROW!

(OR YOU CAN JUST WRITE OR DRAW SOMETHING SILLY DOWN BELOW AND GO TO BED SMILING.)

PLANS FOR TOMORROW/TO DO LIST:

"The secret of getting ahead is getting started. The secret of getting started is breaking your complex overwhelming tasks into manageable tasks, and then starting on the first one."(5) ~Mark Twain

Date ___/___/20__

STRESSFUL MOMENTS:

_____

_____

_____

HAPPY MOMENTS:

_____

_____

_____

PLAN AHEAD TODAY TO MINIMIZE YOUR STRESS TOMORROW!
(OR YOU CAN JUST WRITE OR DRAW SOMETHING SILLY DOWN BELOW AND GO TO BED SMILING.)

PLANS FOR TOMORROW/TO DO LIST::

"Take a deep breath. It's just a bad day, not a bad life."(10)

Date ___/___/20__

STRESSFUL MOMENTS:

_____

_____

_____

HAPPY MOMENTS:

_____

_____

_____

PLAN AHEAD TODAY TO MINIMIZE YOUR STRESS TOMORROW!
(OR YOU CAN JUST WRITE OR DRAW SOMETHING SILLY DOWN BELOW AND GO TO BED SMILING.)
PLANS FOR TOMORROW/TO DO LIST:

"Holding on to anger is like drinking poison and expecting the other person to die."(10)

~Buddha

Date ___/___/20__

STRESSFUL MOMENTS:

_____

_____

_____

HAPPY MOMENTS:

_____

_____

_____

PLAN AHEAD TODAY TO MINIMIZE YOUR STRESS TOMORROW!
(OR YOU CAN JUST WRITE OR DRAW SOMETHING SILLY DOWN BELOW AND GO TO BED SMILING.)
PLANS FOR TOMORROW/TO DO LIST:

"Whatever is begun in anger ends in shame."(10)   ~Benjamin Franklin

Date ___/___/20__

STRESSFUL MOMENTS:

_____

_____

_____

HAPPY MOMENTS:

_____

_____

_____

PLAN AHEAD TODAY TO MINIMIZE YOUR STRESS TOMORROW!
(OR YOU CAN JUST WRITE OR DRAW SOMETHING SILLY DOWN BELOW AND GO TO BED SMILING.)
PLANS FOR TOMORROW/TO DO LIST:

"The third-rate mind is only happy when it is thinking with the majority. The second-rate mind is only happy when it is thinking with the minority. The first-rate mind is only happy when it is thinking."(10)

~A.A.Milne

Date ___/___/20__

STRESSFUL MOMENTS:

_____

_____

_____

HAPPY MOMENTS:

_____

_____

_____

PLAN AHEAD TODAY TO MINIMIZE YOUR STRESS TOMORROW!

(OR YOU CAN JUST WRITE OR DRAW SOMETHING SILLY DOWN BELOW AND GO TO BED SMILING.)

PLANS FOR TOMORROW/TO DO LIST:

Never stop chasing your dream, because sometimes what you need is just one more step.

Date ___ / ___ /20__

STRESSFUL MOMENTS:

_____

_____

_____

HAPPY MOMENTS:

_____

_____

_____

PLAN AHEAD TODAY TO MINIMIZE YOUR STRESS TOMORROW!
(OR YOU CAN JUST WRITE OR DRAW SOMETHING SILLY DOWN BELOW AND GO TO BED SMILING.)
PLANS FOR TOMORROW/TO DO LIST:

> "Promise me you'll always remember: You're braver than you believe, and stronger than you seem, and smarter than you think."(10)
>
> ~A.A.Milne

Date ___/___/20__

STRESSFUL MOMENTS:

_____

_____

_____

HAPPY MOMENTS:

_____

_____

_____

PLAN AHEAD TODAY TO MINIMIZE YOUR STRESS TOMORROW!

(OR YOU CAN JUST WRITE OR DRAW SOMETHING SILLY DOWN BELOW AND GO TO BED SMILING.)

PLANS FOR TOMORROW/TO DO LIST:

"There are two ways of being happy: We must either diminish our wants or increase our means. Either may do - the result is the same; and it is for each man to decide for himself and to do that which happens to be easier."(10)   ~Benjamin Franklin

Date ___/___/20__

STRESSFUL MOMENTS:

_____

_____

_____

HAPPY MOMENTS:

_____

_____

_____

PLAN AHEAD TODAY TO MINIMIZE YOUR STRESS TOMORROW!
(OR YOU CAN JUST WRITE OR DRAW SOMETHING SILLY DOWN BELOW AND GO TO BED SMILING.)
PLANS FOR TOMORROW/TO DO LIST:

"Be slow in choosing a friend, slower in changing."(10)

~Benjamin Franklin

Date ___/___/20__

STRESSFUL MOMENTS:

_____

_____

_____

HAPPY MOMENTS:

_____

_____

_____

PLAN AHEAD TODAY TO MINIMIZE YOUR STRESS TOMORROW!

(OR YOU CAN JUST WRITE OR DRAW SOMETHING SILLY DOWN BELOW AND GO TO BED SMILING.)

PLANS FOR TOMORROW/TO DO LIST:

"Happiness depends more on the inward disposition of mind than on outward circumstances."(10)   ~Benjamin Franklin

Date ___ / ___ /20 __

STRESSFUL MOMENTS:

_____

_____

_____

HAPPY MOMENTS:

_____

_____

_____

PLAN AHEAD TODAY TO MINIMIZE YOUR STRESS TOMORROW!

(OR YOU CAN JUST WRITE OR DRAW SOMETHING SILLY DOWN BELOW AND GO TO BED SMILING.)

PLANS FOR TOMORROW/TO DO LIST:

Do at least ONE small thing just for YOU every day!

Date ___/___/20__

STRESSFUL MOMENTS:

_____

_____

_____

HAPPY MOMENTS:

_____

_____

_____

PLAN AHEAD TODAY TO MINIMIZE YOUR STRESS TOMORROW!
(OR YOU CAN JUST WRITE OR DRAW SOMETHING SILLY DOWN BELOW AND GO TO BED SMILING.)
PLANS FOR TOMORROW/TO DO LIST:

Don't stress out over things you can't control.

Date ___ / ___ /20 __

STRESSFUL MOMENTS:

_____

_____

_____

HAPPY MOMENTS:

_____

_____

_____

PLAN AHEAD TODAY TO MINIMIZE YOUR STRESS TOMORROW!
(OR YOU CAN JUST WRITE OR DRAW SOMETHING SILLY DOWN BELOW AND GO TO BED SMILING.)
PLANS FOR TOMORROW/TO DO LIST:

> **"Everything happens for a reason. Sometimes good things fall apart so better thing can come together."**(10)
> ~Marilyn Monroe

Date ___/___/20__

STRESSFUL MOMENTS:

_____

_____

_____

HAPPY MOMENTS:

_____

_____

_____

PLAN AHEAD TODAY TO MINIMIZE YOUR STRESS TOMORROW!

(OR YOU CAN JUST WRITE OR DRAW SOMETHING SILLY DOWN BELOW AND GO TO BED SMILING.)

PLANS FOR TOMORROW/TO DO LIST:

"Carry out a random act of kindness with no expectation of reward, safe in the knowledge that one day someone might do the same for you."(5)

~Princess Diana

Date ___/___/20__

STRESSFUL MOMENTS:

_____

_____

_____

HAPPY MOMENTS:

_____

_____

_____

PLAN AHEAD TODAY TO MINIMIZE YOUR STRESS TOMORROW!
(OR YOU CAN JUST WRITE OR DRAW SOMETHING SILLY DOWN BELOW AND GO TO BED SMILING.)

PLANS FOR TOMORROW/TO DO LIST:

"A positive thinker sees the invisible, feels the intangible, achieves the impossible."(10)

~Anonymous

Date ___/___/20__

STRESSFUL MOMENTS:

_____

_____

_____

HAPPY MOMENTS:

_____

_____

_____

PLAN AHEAD TODAY TO MINIMIZE YOUR STRESS TOMORROW!

(OR YOU CAN JUST WRITE OR DRAW SOMETHING SILLY DOWN BELOW AND GO TO BED SMILING.)

PLANS FOR TOMORROW/TO DO LIST:

"The secret of getting ahead is getting started."(2)   ~Agatha Christie

Date ___ / ___ /20__

STRESSFUL MOMENTS:

_____

_____

_____

HAPPY MOMENTS:

_____

_____

_____

PLAN AHEAD TODAY TO MINIMIZE YOUR STRESS TOMORROW!
(OR YOU CAN JUST WRITE OR DRAW SOMETHING SILLY DOWN BELOW AND GO TO BED SMILING.)
PLANS FOR TOMORROW/TO DO LIST:

A negative mind will never give you a positive life. Stay positive. Just smile!

Date ___/___/20__

STRESSFUL MOMENTS:

_____

_____

_____

HAPPY MOMENTS:

_____

_____

_____

PLAN AHEAD TODAY TO MINIMIZE YOUR STRESS TOMORROW!
(OR YOU CAN JUST WRITE OR DRAW SOMETHING SILLY DOWN BELOW AND GO TO BED SMILING.)
PLANS FOR TOMORROW/TO DO LIST:

> **"Your vision will become clear only when you can look into your own heart. Who looks outside, dreams; who looks inside, awakes."**(5)
>
> ~Carl Jung

Date ___/___/20__

STRESSFUL MOMENTS:

_____

_____

_____

HAPPY MOMENTS:

_____

_____

_____

PLAN AHEAD TODAY TO MINIMIZE YOUR STRESS TOMORROW!

(OR YOU CAN JUST WRITE OR DRAW SOMETHING SILLY DOWN BELOW AND GO TO BED SMILING.)

PLANS FOR TOMORROW/TO DO LIST:

"I am not what happened to me; I am what I choose to be."(5)

~Carl Jung

Date ___/___/20__

STRESSFUL MOMENTS:

_____

_____

_____

HAPPY MOMENTS:

_____

_____

_____

PLAN AHEAD TODAY TO MINIMIZE YOUR STRESS TOMORROW!

(OR YOU CAN JUST WRITE OR DRAW SOMETHING SILLY DOWN BELOW AND GO TO BED SMILING.)

PLANS FOR TOMORROW/TO DO LIST:

"The word 'happy' would lose its meaning if it were not balanced by sadness."(5)

~Carl Jung

Date ___/___/20__

STRESSFUL MOMENTS:

_____

_____

_____

HAPPY MOMENTS:

_____

_____

_____

PLAN AHEAD TODAY TO MINIMIZE YOUR STRESS TOMORROW!
(OR YOU CAN JUST WRITE OR DRAW SOMETHING SILLY DOWN BELOW AND GO TO BED SMILING.)

PLANS FOR TOMORROW/TO DO LIST:

Congrats!!! YOU did it!!!

You just finished YOUR Journal! Treat yourself to something nice. Don't forget: **the end is a new beginning!**

The Mother and Daughter team is confident to say that by now you are in much better control of your emotions and life in general!

We are kindly asking you to **share your results** with the people you love and respect.
Also, it would be **greatly appreciated** if you could give your feedback and share your own experiences with others by writing a review. We would love to know how The Stress-Less Guide changed YOUR own life.

And the most important thing:

We would like to thank YOU!!! Yes, You and only You!!!

Without you doing all the work, the changes in your life and other people's lives wouldn't be possible. With your help, we will improve the quality of life of so many people and helpless animals.
P.S. We are hoping that by now you're holding a new copy in your hands so you can continue to enjoy your Stress-Less life.

REFERENCES

1. *Wikipedia: The Free Encyclopedia.* Wikimedia Foundation, Inc. Web. https://www.wikipedia.org/.

2. Patel, Gunvanta. *Quotes – Daily Inspirational and Motivational App. Computer Software. Apple App Store. Vers. 2.2*

3. "Quotations." *Quotes Wiki,* www.quotes.wiki/.

4. Mercola, J. "How Stress Affects Your Body, and Simple Techniques to Reduce Stress and Develop Greater Resilience." 10 Apr. 2016. https://articles.mercola.com/sites/articles/archive/2016/04/10/how-stress-affects-body.aspx.

5. "Famous Quotes at BrainyQuote." *BrainyQuote,* Xplore, www.brainyquote.com/.

6. Mercola, J. "8 Stress-Busting Tips from Experts." 7, Nov 2013. https://articles.mercola.com/sites/articles/archive/2013/11/07/8-stress-management-tips.aspx.

7. Mercola, J. "Stress Doesn't Stay in Your Head." 12, Mar. 2015. https://articles.mercola.com/sites/articles/archive/2015/03/12/chronic-stress.aspx.

8. "IquoteTank." *Iquotetank,* iquotetank.info/.

9. "Quotes.net." *Ukrainian President Petro Poroshenko Quotes,* www.quotes.net/.

10. "Pinterest." *Pinterest,* www.pinterest.com/.

www.ingramcontent.com/pod-product-compliance
Lightning Source LLC
Chambersburg PA
CBHW081654270326
41933CB00017B/3163